PERSON-IN-ENVIRONMENT SYSTEM MANUAL

2ND EDITION

by

James M. Karls and Maura E. O' Keefe

NASW PRESS

National Association of Social Workers
Washington, DC

James J. Kelly, PhD, ACSW, President
Elizabeth J. Clark, PhD, ACSW, MPH, Executive Dire

Cheryl Bradley, Publisher
Marcia Roman, Managing Editor, Journals and Books
Kathie Baker, Copy Editor

Interior design by Chris Phillips, Circle Graphics, Columbia, MD.
Cover design by Suzani Pavone, Eye to Eye Design, Bristow, VA.
Printed by Victor Graphics, Baltimore, MD.

Library of Congress Cataloging-in-Publication data
Person-in-environment system manual/(edited by) James M. Karls & Maura E. O'Keefe—2nd ed.
        . cm.
    Includes bibliographical references and indexes.
    ISBN 13: 978-0-87101-379-8 (alk. Paper)
    ISBN 10: 0-87101-379-7
  1. Person-in-environment system. I. Karls, James M., 1927-   II. O'Keefe, Maura E.
HV43.5 P47 2007
361.1014—dc22   2007043242

Contents

Foreword

It has been over 10 years since *The Person-in-Environment System* (PIE) book and manual were first published by NASW Press. The hopes and expectations of those involved in developing the PIE system were both modest and ambitious. Working as a task force of the National Association of Social Workers, their hope was that PIE would be the **beginning** of a process by which the profession of social work would develop a diagnostic and assessment system that truly reflected its unique role in the human services field. It was also expected that PIE would be an **initial** step in developing a classification and diagnostic system that could be used in all fields of practice and that PIE would need to be modified and added to as it was put into practice.

The acceptance of PIE among social work colleagues has far exceeded the expectations of the task force that first put it together. Without a great deal of advertising, more than 15,000 copies have been sold in the United States. It is not a big number by pop novel standards but a best seller among social work books.

The most surprising event has been the discovery of PIE by social workers around the world. There are official translations into Spanish, French, Greek, Hungarian, Japanese, and Korean; and translations are being developed for German, Hebrew, and some South African languages. It is widely used in Canada and has been used in research projects in Australia and other countries. PIE has struck a chord in the hearts and minds of our social work colleagues around the world. We have received numerous suggestions and ideas for improving PIE and have incorporated many of them into this new version of PIE.

Our mission remains the same: to provide the practitioner and researcher a tool by which the problems presented by human services clients can be systematically and comprehensively assessed, described, and addressed and to show social work's unique contribution to the human services field.

We hope those who have been using PIE will find this new version clearer and more useful in their work. The strengths perspective has been enhanced. There have been some changes in the types of discrimination. The numerical coding system has been de-emphasized. And the recording instruments have been developed to allow for full intervention plans and testing of interventions. The software, making recording much simpler in this era, is included in the revision. For those trying PIE the first time we hope that it will help them identify and assess the many and complex issues that clients present and arrive at an intervention plan that will truly help the client.

There have been many who have contributed to this version of the PIE system: Dr. Karin Wandrei who wrote most of the manual copy in the first edition and is now an administrator of a county-wide agency in California; Dick Ramsay in Calgary who continues to work on the development of PIE in Canada; Dr. Joan Keefler in Montreal who has made many suggestions that are incorporated into this version; Deborah Foster in Connecticut who has created some clever systems for recording findings,; Dr Shirley Keller in Ohio who has reviewed and provided constructive suggestions as the revision was in process; Dr. George Appleby in Connecticut whose work on using PIE in assessing discrimination helped us modify that section of PIE; Dr. Wim Roestenburg and his colleague Dr. Rika Swanzen at the University of Johannesburg who have provided feedback on this version of PIE and are working on a children's version; Dean Marilyn Flynn at the University of Southern California who has supported our efforts over time and has facilitated teaching PIE to all MSW students using the PIE software; Kristen Butler who worked on the editing and revision of the worksheet; and there are many, many others who have provided suggestions. We are thankful to them all.

James M. Karls, PhD, LCSW
Clinical Associate Professor
University of Southern California

Maura E. O'Keefe, PhD, LCSW
Associate Professor
University of California, Sacramento

Foreword

Person In Environment (PIE), first published by the NASW Press in 1994, represents social work's unique take on the human condition and provides a starting point for its professionals to improve quality of life within the context of an individual's situation. For a mentally ill person, for example, a social worker doesn't just focus on medications and psychological/psychiatric remediation, but rather casts a wide net to examine all stressors and potential supports including economics, living conditions, training and work availability, family and supplementary services, and advocacy for the individual.

Of critical value to the social work profession, PIE has evolved in its ability to represent how social work differs from other human services disciplines, as well as to provide social workers with a glimpse of an individual's circumstances and options as if they were standing in their clients' shoes.

NASW is proud to sponsor PIE and looks forward to its seeing this ever-changing tool assist social work professionals around the globe.

James J. Kelly
President
NASW

Foreword

I am pleased to be asked again to write a foreword for the PIE Manual.

The first version successfully provided a framework for understanding the unique contribution of social work globally and at the same time provided a how-to map for practitioners in doing our work. This revised edition has the advantage of further experience and use. Feedback from practitioners around the world has been used to refine and enhance this truly brilliant, original and creative concept.

As the former President of the International Federation of Social Workers and the current Ambassador for this organization, I can attest to the importance of the PIE in helping unify and standardize social work practice around the world. Requests for translations have been spontaneous, initiated by social workers in many countries who want to improve their skills and further professionalize their work. The hope has been that PIE would be a culture-friendly instrument, adaptable to many settings, many practice styles and systems and workable with a variety of ethnic clients. Its use from Korea to Hungary to South Africa is testimony that the framers have more than succeeded. In an increasingly fragmented world, PIE expresses the universality of our concern for others and operationalizes the skills we have developed for moving beyond concern into action.

Our clients, our profession, and society thank you – Jim Karls!

Sue Dworak-Peck

Introduction

In human services practice, assessment is the foundation for planning and implementing the interventions that will alleviate the client's distress. The assessment is more than a diagnosis. Because of the complexity of most client situations, the diagnosis of a mental condition or a physical problem is not sufficient to plan or to begin work with the client. And assessment by intuition only focused on the services available from the practitioner or the agency will seldom lead to a good resolution. A careful comprehensive assessment focusing on the needs of the client is more likely to lead to a successful outcome. PIE is the instrument for providing a comprehensive assessment.

The *PIE* (person-in-environment) *Manual* is for those social workers and other human services workers who plan to use the PIE system in their practice, teaching, or research. This *Manual* operationalizes the PIE System. By studying the instructions that follow, those who are familiar with the concepts of person-in-environment should easily be able to use the PIE System in assessing the problems presented by their clients. Careful study of the *Manual* will lead the practitioner to produce a succinct summary of the problem complex and the interventions that may alleviate the client's conditions. Recording instruments in the *Manual* and in the accompanying CompuPIE software help to minimize the amount of time needed to produce a comprehensive written report of case findings.

Practitioners not familiar with the concepts may wish to review the material presented in the *Person-in-Environment System* book available from NASW Press. For those already familiar with the PIE system, it may be useful to be reminded that PIE is a biopsychosocial system that has added the elements of "environment" and "strengths" to the assessment process. PIE is a "holistic" system that gives primacy to the ability of the clients to function in their social roles. Mental and physical health problems and problems in the community are assessed in terms of their effect on the client's ability to live a productive life. Adequate social functioning—the ability to fulfill major social roles as required by the client's culture or community—is the major goal of interventions derived from the PIE assessment. Problems in the environment and in mental and physical health are viewed as influencing social functioning and are thus addressed to the extent that they affect functioning. Added to this mix are the client's strengths that may affect the need for intervention.

PIE is used primarily in the assessment phase of working with a client, although for the researcher it is an instrument for assessing the effects of interventions over time, and for the teacher it is a tool for helping the student understand the complex problems that people bring to health, mental health, and social agencies. And it is an effective instrument for practitioners in evidence-based practice or case management who look for methods to measure the effectiveness of an intervention. For the administrator it can be a data collection tool, which, combined with the numerical coding system that is available in the software program, can provide an ongoing assessment of agency clientele and program effectiveness. It serves to identify, classify, and describe the problems brought to practitioners in private practice, in social agencies, in health and mental health services, and in other setting where social workers and other human service care providers practice.

The PIE system is designed to accommodate not only varied practice settings, but also the various theoretical orientations that may guide the practitioner. The PIE system helps the practitioners collect data on various aspects of the client's condition, then study the complex, and apply the theoretical orientation—psychoanalytic, behavioral, feminist, and so forth—with which they are most comfortable to evaluate the interaction of the elements of the finding. PIE then becomes a good vehicle for testing the effectiveness of various theoretical approaches as it also includes recording outcomes of interventions over time.

The PIE system was developed using problems and issues that mainly concern adults. It is therefore not useful in assessing the problems of young children or adolescents. Practitioners working with families can use the PIE system to assess the problems of individual adults in the family, particularly the parents, to better understand the interactional problems in the family. PIE can be used effectively in assessment of emancipated minors who are facing many of the issues of adults.

Don't be put off by the PIE system's length and complexity. The small amount of time spent learning to use it will soon be paid back with the benefit of producing a thorough and professional assessment. The time now spent recording case findings will be greatly reduced and practitioners will have an assessment document that can guide them through the course of their work with the client. For those social workers in multidisciplinary settings the PIE system clarifies social work's areas of expertise. The PIE system demonstrates social work's expertise in problems in social functioning and problems in the environment. Factor I demonstrates the many kinds of relationship problems that social work, as a profession, was created to address. Factor II identifies the many problems in the social institutions in the community that social work has traditionally addressed. And PIE clarifies that the areas of physical and mental health are shared with other human service professionals (Factor III and Factor IV).

We hope the PIE System will help you sort through the complex issues that your clients bring to you and that both you and your client will be better for using it. Suggestions for improving the system are welcome.

CHAPTER 1

The PIE System

Structure of the PIE System

PIE provides a systematic approach to assessing the social functioning problems and strengths experienced by the clients of social workers and other human service practitioners. When used in practice, it can produce descriptions that are concise, uniform, and easily understood by both clients and practitioners. The PIE system requires that every client be described on each of several dimensions called "factors." Each factor refers to a different class of information. For a classification system to have maximum usefulness, there must be sufficient data to provide an adequate picture of the client, but not so much as to overwhelm or befuddle those who would use the system to plan interventions.

There are four factors in the PIE system. The first two factors constitute the core social work description. The second two factors identify mental and physical health problems using classification systems from other professions. All four factors are needed to provide a comprehensive picture of a client's problems. A Strengths component is also included for each factor. Wherever there is a problem, looking for strengths often can be used as a starting point for intervention. Identification of client strengths may foster hope by focusing on what is or has been successful for the client.

The PIE system describes the client's problem complex in the following format:

Factor I   Social Functioning Problems: type, severity, duration, coping ability and strengths

Factor II   Environmental Problems: severity, duration and resources or strengths

Factor III   Mental Health Problems and Strengths

Factor IV   Physical Health Problems and Strengths

On Factor I the practitioner identifies the client's social role problems. There can be and usually are more than one Factor I problem. The practitioner also identifies each problem's type, the severity of the disruption caused by the problem, the duration of the problem, the client's coping capacity for dealing with each problem and notable or possible client strengths.

On Factor II the practitioner identifies not only the environmental conditions or problems affecting Factor I problems, but also the severity of the disruption caused by each problem and each problem's duration. There can also be more than one Factor II problem. It is also important to identify community strengths or resources

Factors I and II form the core description of a client's social functioning problems and strengths and generally are the primary focus of social work intervention.

Factors III and IV describe the client's mental and physical health condition. These may affect social functioning but are not necessarily the direct focus of the social work practitioner, although many social work practitioners are trained and licensed to treat mental disorders.

This separation of problems into four factors and the primacy given to social role and environmental problems are intended to emphasize the importance of the client's social functioning—a focus that frequently is difficult to maintain when attention is directed to the usually more vivid Factors III and IV. Thus, the social worker's emphasis is on the social role or environmental problems of a client who may also have a mental or physical disorder. Although the primary focus of PIE is not on the mental and physical problems, interventions may and often do include medical and psychological treatment.

Factor III permits the practitioner to indicate any current mental, personality, or developmental disorder or condition that is potentially relevant to the understanding of or intervention with the individual. These conditions are listed on Axes I and II of the *Diagnostic and Statistical Manual of Mental Disorders, 4th Edition-text revision* (DSM-IV-TR) (American Psychiatric Association, 2000). It is assumed that the practitioner is familiar with the use of DSM-IV TR or can obtain consultation on assessing mental disorders. Thus, the use of DSM-IV TR is not discussed in detail in this manual.

Factor IV permits the practitioner to indicate any current physical disorder or condition that is potentially relevant to the understanding or management of the social role or environmental problems of a client. Factor IV is equivalent to Axis III in DSM-IV-TR. These are the conditions exclusive of the mental disorders section of the *International Classification of Diseases-10 Revision-Clinical Modification* (ICD-10-CM) (World Health Organization, 2005). Some practitioners may wish to use the newly developing International Classification of Functioning, Disability and Health (ICF) (World Heath Organization, 2007), which complements the ICD-10. The social worker should inquire routinely about any significant physical problems and record the results of this inquiry on Factor IV. As a professional who is not licensed to make physical diagnoses, the social worker should note the source of the information. For example, the worker might record the results of an intake evaluation and note on Factor IV "Diabetes (by report of the client)," or "Asthma (diagnosed by Dr. X)," or "Client reports no physical problems."

In some instances, a client's physical condition may be an important source of social role or environmental problems (for example, AIDS in a client with a Lover Role Problem, loss type). In another instance the physical disorder may not be the source of the client's problems, but it may be important in planning an overall intervention strategy (for example, genital herpes in a person with a Spouse Role Problem, ambivalence type). In yet another instance, the practitioner may wish to note significant associated physical findings (for example, history of heart attacks in a client with a Worker Role Problem, loss type). The practitioner should refer to the International Classification of Diseases (ICD-10) for further information pertaining to coding on this factor. If ICD-10 is unavailable, the practitioner may describe the physical disorder in lay language (for example, severe asthma as reported by client).

REFERENCES

American Psychiatric Association. (2000). *Diagnostic and statistical manual of mental disorders* (4th ed.-text rev.). Washington, DC: American Psychiatric Press.

World Health Organization. (2007). *International classification of diseases-10 revision-clinical modification* Available at: http://www.who.int/classifications/apps/icd/icd10online/

World Health Organization. (2001). *International classification of functioning, disability and health.* Available from: www.disabilitaincifre.it/documenti/ICF_18.pdf.

CHAPTER 2

How to Use PIE in Practice

Ideally we conduct and record an assessment that covers all the major aspects of a client's functioning. This task consumes time and can feel burdensome, especially for the conscientious. The PIE System helps to sort and classify the complex data our client may present in a timely and efficient way so necessary in the hurried atmosphere of today's workplace.

Do not be put off by the PIE System's length and complexity. The small amount of time spent learning to use it will soon be paid back, with the benefit of thorough and professional results.

General Guidelines

The following are the general guidelines, the practitioner needs to consider when using the PIE System.

Return to Optimal Social Functioning. In the philosophy underlying the PIE System, the primary goal is to help clients live their lives as fully as possible—to function as well as possible and deal effectively with environmental and physical and mental health conditions. The PIE system helps both you and your client achieve a clear, comprehensive picture of what is needed to reach this goal. Also, the PIE system helps reduce the power barrier between client and social worker by placing the social worker in the role of partner or guide.

Terms and Concepts. Before recording case findings, be certain you understand the terms and concepts used in the PIE system. Consult the PIE Manual for descriptions and definitions of the terms used. The PIE Book can be consulted if you have questions about the concepts and theories utilized in the PIE system.

Hands-Free Interviews. In most cases, findings are recorded **after** the initial assessment interview(s),

which may be conducted in the practitioner's personal style. This allows for a freer presentation by the client and less distraction for the clinician.

PIE is NOT an Interview Guide. Neither the PIE Worksheet nor the CompuPIE software program should be used as an interview guide. Work with your client in your usual style using the theoretical framework that suits you best.

Unrestricted Problem Identification. You may record as many problems as are identified in the assessment. In most cases more than one problem will be found. However, there need not be a problem on each factor.

Strengths Perspective. PIE encourages practitioners to look beyond problems to identify the client's coping capacities and strengths as well as assets and resources in the environment. This will help you to evaluate the client's potential for helping himself/herself and for using environmental resources.

Planning Interventions. The PIE System includes an element for recording proposed interventions and expected outcomes useful in case management or for evidence based practice. The manual provides a partial list of common interventions to facilitate planning.

Adult Version. This edition of the PIE System is for use with adults, defined as people 18 years old or older or an emancipated minor under 18. Assessment of children's conditions is often facilitated by using a PIE assessment with the parent or guardian of the child.

Tools for Recording

The CompuPIE software program and the PIE Worksheet will help you record the findings of your assessment.

1. CompuPIE is a copyrighted software program for recording assessments based on the PIE system.

The CompuPIE software compiles findings into a PIE Assessment Summary more easily than is possible manually. CompuPIE requires the availability of Microsoft Access.

2. The PIE System Worksheet is a printed form that contains all the elements of the PIE System. It is used to record findings manually. The PIE System Worksheet is not copyrighted and may be reproduced as many times as necessary. (See pages 34–46)

The Assessment Process Using the PIE System

As described in chapter 1 a PIE System assessment encompasses four areas called "Factors"

Factor I	Social Role and Relationship Functioning
Factor II	Environmental Conditions affecting Client Functioning (Social Support Systems)
Factor III	Mental Health Functioning
Factor IV	Physical Health Functioning

For each PIE factor there are fours steps in the assessment:

(1) Problem Identification
(2) Identification of Strengths and Resources
(3) Intervention Plan
(4) Assessment Summary

The succinct formula of Problem Identification, Strengths Identification, and Recommended Intervention applied to each of the four PIE factors will help clarify your thinking about your client and the client's environment and the effects of mental and physical health conditions. And, when you are familiar with the terms and concepts, you will be able to record an assessment in record time using the CompuPIE software or slightly longer using the manual PIE System Worksheet. You will be pleased with how complete and clear your assessment is and how easily colleagues and clients can understand it.

The description of the assessment process that follows gives a step-by-step picture of the process. Because the steps are similar in each Factor there is some repetition. To do a thorough assessment you will need to take these steps. Once you have learned the procedure the process will run quickly and smoothly. The items in

parentheses after each question refer to the locale in the PIE Worksheet and CompuPIE where the finding is recorded

Factor I: Social Role and Relationship Functioning

Step 1: Problem Identification

Factor I identifies the problem(s) that the client is experiencing in social role and relationship functioning. The PIE system asks you to identify:

(1) In what social role(s) or relationship(s) is the client having a problem (Role)?
(2) What kind of problem is it (Type)?
(3) How significant is the problem (Severity)?
(4) How long has the problem existed (Duration)?

Step 2: Identification of Strengths and Resources

In the course of the assessment the practitioner using the PIE System will have identified strengths and resources in two areas:

(1) the client's ability to cope with each problem identified and
(2) the presence of positive social roles or relationships. (For example, there may be **somewhat inadequate** ability to cope with a problem in the occupational role but **outstanding** functioning in relationship with a spouse or family member)

In regard to Strengths and Resources the PIE system asks you to identify:

(1) how well the client can cope with each social role problem at the present time (Coping Ability)
(2) in what social role or relationship is the client showing a strength that may be useful in working on the presenting problem(s) (Other Strengths)

Step 3: Intervention Plan

In following the PIE System format you will have entered, either using the CompuPIE software or the PIE Worksheet, a recommended intervention and other data for each problem or condition you identified on Factor I. You will have recorded:

(1) A possible goal related to this problem (for example, reconciliation, return to employment)
(2) What intervention you recommend (Intervention)?
(3) Who is to work with the client (Refer to)?
(4) What is the expected outcome? (Outcome)

Step 4: Assessment Summary

A crucial next step consists of transferring the problems and conditions identified in Factors I to the Assessment Summary and Intervention Plan part of the PIE System Worksheet (refer to the accompanying PIE Assessment Worksheet for the specifics on this). You will have answered:

(1) How many and what kind of social role and relationship problems have been identified?
(2) What strengths have been identified?
(3) What interventions are recommended?
(4) What practitioner or agency is expected to work with the client?
(5) What is the goal of the intervention and the expected outcome?

Factor II: Environmental Situations (Social Support Systems)

Step 1: Problem Identification

In PIE the term "environment" or "environmental situations" refers to natural helping networks, social support systems, and social institutions that exist in most communities.

Factor II identifies problems the client is experiencing within any of the six System Types used in PIE (Basic Needs; Education and Training; Judicial and Legal; Health, Safety, and Social Services; Voluntary Association; and Affectional Support). These are problems in the client's **current** environment that affect social functioning. In Step 1 the PIE System asks:

(1) Is the client experiencing a problem in any of the environmental systems? Which system is it? Basic Needs; Education and Training; Judicial and Legal; Health, Safety, and Social Services; Voluntary Association; or Affectional Support? In what part or aspect of the system is the problem located? (Type)
(2) What kind of problem is it? (Type) Is it absence of shelter, lack of education facilities, lack of confi-

dence in police services, inaccessible health services, no community support groups, or other type listed in the PIE Manual and on the PIE Worksheet?
(3) How significant is the problem (Severity)
(4) How long has this situation been a factor in the client's life (Duration)?
(5) Is the client having problems in environmental situations because of who they are or their status in society (Discrimination).

Discrimination in the community social support system due to age, sexual orientation, disability status, and so forth, is a special category in Factor II. When discrimination is detected in any of the situations in Factor II, it is recorded in the Factor II statement along with a recommended intervention. Refer to the Discrimination Index for a list of types of discrimination.

Step 2: Resources

In Step 2 the PIE System identifies the agencies, institutions or social support systems that can provide resources or opportunities to the client (Resources). It determines whether there are services in the community that can help with the client's current problems. Using the type listings on the PIE System Worksheet you can identify a community resource and can provide detailed information about it in the Narrative and Comments Section of the PIE Worksheet. For example, a well functioning housing program can help with the client who is homeless and would be entered on the Worksheet as Basic Needs, Shelter. An accessible mental health service would be entered as Health/Mental Health. An accessible religious group can provide for a client's spiritual needs and would be entered under Voluntary Associations, Religious Groups.

The PIE System question addressed is:

(1) In which of the systems in Factor II are there resources/strengths to address the client's situation? (Resources)

Step 3: Intervention Plan

As in Factor I, following the PIE System format, you will have entered, either on the PIE Worksheet or the CompuPIE software, a recommended intervention and other case management data that might be used for each problem or condition you identified on Factor II. You will have recorded:

(1) What is the recommended intervention (Intervention)?
(2) Who is to work with the client (Refer to)?
(3) What is the goal of the intervention (Goal)?
(4) What is the expected outcome? (Outcome)

Step 4: Assessment Summary

Problems and situations identified in Factor II are transferred to the Assessment Summary and Intervention Plan part of the PIE System Worksheet. Practitioner findings answer the questions:

(1) How many and what kind of Environmental Situation problems have been identified?
(2) What community resources potentially useful in helping the client have been identified?
(3) What interventions are recommended?
(4) What practitioner or agency is expected to work with the client?
(5) What is the goal of the intervention
(6) What is the expected outcome?

Factor III: Mental Health Functioning

Factor III describes the client's Mental Health Functioning using either the DSM (Diagnostic and Statistical Manual) or other mental health diagnostic systems such as the International Classification of Diseases or International Classification of Functioning to describe the client's mental health condition.

Step 1: Problem Identification

The PIE System asks:

(1) Is there a clinical syndrome? What is the DSM Axis or other diagnostic system diagnosis? (Diagnosis)
(2) Is there an enduring characteristic? Is there a personality disorder and/or mental retardation using the DSM Axis II or other diagnostic system diagnosis? (Diagnosis)
(3) How significant is the problem? (Severity)
(4) How long has the client had this condition? (Duration)

Step 2: Strengths

The PIE System asks:

(1) How well does the client cope with the mental health condition? (Coping)
(2) Are there notable mental health strengths (for example, intelligence, resilience, self identity, spiritual awareness) (Other Strengths)

Step 3: Intervention Plan

The PIE System asks:

(1) What is the goal of the intervention (Goal)?
(2) What is the recommended intervention (Intervention)?
(3) Who is to work with the client (Refer to)?
(4) What is the expected outcome (Outcome?

Step 4: Assessment Summary

Problems and situations identified in Factors III are transferred to the Assessment Summary and Intervention Plan part of the PIE System Worksheet. Practitioner findings answer the questions:

(1) How many and what kind of mental health conditions have been identified?
(2) How severe is each?
(3) How long has the client had the condition?
(4) What is the goal of the intervention
(5) What interventions are recommended?
(6) What practitioner or agency is expected to work with the client?
(7) What is the expected outcome?

Factor IV: Physical Health Functioning

Factor IV describes the client's Physical Health Functioning by enumerating the physical health problems identified by the client or others.

Step 1: Problem Identification

The PIE System asks:

(1) Is there a medical condition as diagnosed by a physician or other licensed medical practitioner (Diagnosed Condition)?
(2) What additional health conditions does the client or others report? (Other conditions)

(3) How significant is each condition? (Severity)

(4) How long has the client had each condition? (Duration)

Step 2: Strengths and Resources

The PIE System asks:

(1) How well does the client cope with each physical health condition(s) (Coping)?

(2) Are there notable physical health strengths (for example, vigor, stamina) (Strength)?

Step 3: Intervention

The PIE System asks:

(1) What is the recommended intervention for each condition (Intervention)?

(2) Who is to work with the client (Refer to)?

(3) What is the goal of the intervention (Goal)?

(4) What is the expected outcome (Outcome)?

Step 4: Assessment Summary

Problems and situations identified in Factors IV are transferred to the Assessment Summary and Intervention Plan part of the PIE System Worksheet. Practitioner findings answer the questions:

(1) How many and what kind of physical health conditions have been identified?

(2) What interventions are recommended?

(3) What practitioner or agency is expected to work with the client?

(4) What is the goal of the interventions?

(5) What is the expected outcome?

Summing It All Up

The Assessment Summary and Intervention Plan

The combined findings from all four factors provide you with the comprehensive picture that is the goal of the PIE assessment process. The beauty of the PIE System is in its helping you take a mass of complex client information, sort it out, and then create a succinct yet comprehensive picture of the client's situation. With a clearer focus on problems, strengths, resources, and possible interventions, the task of deciding how, when, and where to begin constructive work with the client is that much easier. You will be able to decide more clearly the issues that can be dealt with by the client without practitioner help, those that you or your agency can address, and those that might be referred to others. Both the PIE Worksheet and the CompuPIE software lend themselves to modifying findings as new information is received about the client's condition or situation

To create a comprehensive yet succinct summary of assessment findings you use the "Assessment Summary and Intervention Plan" document (p.xx in the manual). Enter your findings on the worksheet or on the CompuPIE program. The resulting document becomes both the case record and the plan for proceeding in work with the client or, in the case of Factor II, with the environment.

Setting priorities for intervention can be facilitated by using the severity and duration indicators. PIE helps the practitioner plan interventions more effectively by identifying those problems or conditions that are of high priority and those less urgent. A problem of recent onset with high severity is usually of higher priority than a problem of long duration and of low severity. Assessing strengths can be an important tool for mobilizing capacities and competences in both the individual and his/her environment.

Case History, Dynamics, and Comments

Because of the succinctness of the PIE Summary and Intervention plan, some practitioners find it useful to provide background history, explain the dynamics in the situation from their theoretical perspective, or note issues to explore in future work with the client. The worksheet provides space for this under the title: Clinical Notes, Case Analysis, and Interpretation of Findings.

3 CHAPTER

Factor I: Social Role and Relationship Functioning

Most clients present themselves or are referred for help because they are having difficulties functioning in their social roles. A person's social role can be defined in terms of fulfilling a position in society such as a parent, spouse, student, or employee. Tradition, law, and both societal and family values define the content of roles. Although the major functions of roles are similar across cultures, the ways in which these functions are carried out may vary from culture to culture and from subgroup to subgroup within a specific culture.

Social Role Descriptions and Codes

Listed below are the various social roles used in the PIE system. They are grouped into four major categories: Family Roles, Other Interpersonal Roles, Occupational Roles, and Special Life Situation Roles. For each of the four categories, descriptions of social role problems are listed with illustrative examples to clarify the concepts. These examples should encompass most social role problems that are likely to be encountered in practice. Whenever possible, the practitioner should use a specific social role category rather than the "Other" code.

Social Roles

Family Roles
Parent
Spouse
Child (Adult)
Sibling
Extended Family

Other Interpersonal Roles
Lover
Friend
Neighbor
Member
Other

Occupational Roles
Paid Worker
Homemaker
Volunteer
Student
Other

Special Life Situation Roles
Consumer
Caregiver
Inpatient/Client
Outpatient/Client
Probationer/Parolee
Prisoner
Legal Immigrant
Undocumented Immigrant
Refugee Immigrant
Other

Definition of Social Roles

Family Roles

Family roles are social roles that are played out in the context of a family setting in which the individuals are linked by blood, law, or informal arrangements.

Parent. Parents/caregivers hold the major responsibilities for nurturing and socializing each successive generation. These responsibilities include providing necessities such as shelter, food and safety. The role also includes providing guidance, support, and love; assisting with developmental tasks; transmitting family and cultural lore; and providing a family and cultural identity.

A person assuming Parental Role responsibility may be a natural parent, stepparent, adoptive parent, or someone legally or informally assuming the responsibilities for a specific minor. Who exercises the Parent Role and how he or she fulfills its responsibilities may vary from family to family and from culture to culture. In most societies, the parent has legal responsibility for the welfare of the child and cultural expectations of minimal parenting requirements are prescribed by law.

The following are examples of Parent Role Problems:

- A parent who is having problems with a rebellious teenager.
- A father who loses contact with his children after a divorce.
- A foster parent who is distressed when a child is removed from his or her care.
- A lesbian mother who is worried about her child being teased at school for having two mothers.

Spouse. The Spouse Role encompasses the responsibilities and expectations assigned to each of two people who have formed a legal, religious, or private union for the purposes of basic physical and economic security, emotional and sexual gratification, social recognition, companionship, and in some instances, procreation.

The following are examples of Spouse Role Problems:

- An individual who feels disconnected from his/her partner emotionally, psychologically, or physically.
- A person who is depressed after a divorce.
- A man who is an alcoholic and physically abusive to his wife.
- A woman who is angry that her live-in female partner is unwilling to be monogamous.

Child (Adult). The PIE system is limited to the classification of the social role problems of adults. Thus, the Child (Adult) Role category refers to adults who are experiencing problems in their relationship with their parents. However, performance of the Child Role is not dependent on the presence of parents.

The following are examples of Child (Adult) Role Problems an adult might experience:

- A 63-year-old woman who is overwhelmed with the care of her aging mother.
- A 25-year-old man who is fearful of his stepfather who molested him when he was 10 years old.
- A 28-year-old gay man who is ambivalent about "coming out" to his parents.
- A 35-year-old woman who has a conflicted relationship with her mother, which dates from her mother not believing that she was raped by an uncle.

Sibling. Sibling Role problems refers to adults who experience a problem in relation to brothers and sisters. Siblings may share one or more common parents or stepparents. They may include biological, adoptive, step or surrogate offspring. In most cultures, sex and birth order determine role expectations. The following are examples of Sibling Role Problems:

- A person who is experiencing conflict with her sibling over the division of their parents' estate.
- A 49-year-old woman who is fighting with her 53-year-old brother about his excessive drinking.
- A 30-year-old male who feels obligated to care for his sister's children because she is an irresponsible parent.

Extended Family. The Extended Family Role is reserved for someone who, by blood ties or by formal or informal agreement, is accepted as a member of the nuclear or extended family. This role would include someone who serves in the role of grandparent, godparent, aunt, uncle, cousin, or in-law, but also would include spouses, grandparents, and other relatives from previous marriages. The type of Other Family Role should be specified in the listing.

The following are examples of Extended Family Role Problems:

- A woman who dislikes the woman her son has married (mother-in-law role)
- A grandmother who loses contact with her grandchildren after a divorce (grandmother role)
- A long-term family friend who is treated as an uncle by the family, but is then ignored by other members of the family because he is not related by blood (uncle role).
- A godmother who does not fulfill her expected responsibilities.

Other Interpersonal Roles

Interpersonal roles are social roles that are played out in interpersonal relationships between individuals who are not members of the same family. They include Lover, Friend, Neighbor, and Member.

Lover. The Lover Role denotes an intimate sexual or potentially sexual relationship between individuals of the same or the opposite sex. It includes dating and courting, but it excludes living together and having a commitment to a long-term relationship. Lovers who live together and are committed to a long-term relationship would be placed into the Spouse Role.

The following are examples of Lover Role Problems:

- A woman who is questioning whether she should move in with her boyfriend.
- A transgender individual who is fighting with his lover about his refusal to "come out" to his family about their relationship
- A woman who feels that she is constantly getting into love relationships with "losers."

Friend. In the Friend Role a person maintains a relationship with another person of the same or the opposite sex for the purpose of mutual emotional and spiritual support and companionship. The role usually does not include a sexual relationship because this would be included in the Lover Role.

The following are examples of Friend Role Problems:

- A woman who is upset that her best friend is ignoring her since she got involved with a new boyfriend.
- A man who is uncertain how to handle a situation involving a couple, both of whom are his friends and who are undergoing a difficult custody battle.
- A woman who is having an argument with a friend who has not returned money lent to her.

Neighbor. The Neighbor Role is primarily a function of geographic proximity resulting in occasional contact between people, usually less frequently than between friends. The basic responsibility of the role is to preserve the health and safety of the shared living environment. Neighbors may also serve as a source of support in a crisis.

The following are examples of Neighbor Role Problems:

- A person who is concerned that his neighbor is selling drugs out of his house.
- A person who is angry because neighbors play loud music all hours of the night and fears confronting them.

- A woman who feels isolated in her new neighborhood because she does not know anyone.

Member. Voluntary affiliation and participation with a group of individuals associated for a common purpose and adhering to mutually agreed-upon beliefs or regulations are the primary characteristics of the Member Role. The specific responsibilities and expectations of the role vary according to the purpose and structure of the group, which can be organized for political, religious, social, recreational, professional, or other reasons.

The following are examples of Member Role Problems:

- A person who is ambivalent regarding whether to run for office in a professional association.
- A man who is distressed by the internal conflict in his church group.
- A woman who is concerned that she may be asked to leave her professional organization when it is discovered that she has been embezzling funds.

Other. Other Interpersonal Role should be used to describe an interpersonal role problem that does not involve Family, Occupational, or Special Life Situation Roles and does not fall into the other categories in this section. In the listing, the practitioner should specify the type of interpersonal role.

The following are examples of Other Interpersonal Role Problems:

- An amateur baseball player who is always arguing with the umpire (athlete role).
- A man who is upset because he has to undergo an audit by the Internal Revenue Service (citizen role).
- A woman who is depressed because of the death of her dog (pet owner role).

Occupational Roles

Occupational roles are those roles performed in the paid or unpaid economy or by students in academic institutions.

Paid Worker. The Paid Worker Role includes activities that a person performs to acquire economic resources. The paid worker may be employed outside or in the home. Unemployed and retired people may be included in this role designation if the situation causing discomfort is associated with the loss of or change in the worker role.

The following are examples of Paid Worker Role-Economic Problems:

- A man who is distressed about his impending retirement.
- A man who feels insulted and treated unfairly by his employer.
- An individual who has been reprimanded by his supervisor for erratic attendance, drinking on the job, and poor performance.

Homemaker. The Homemaker Role includes all responsibilities and expectations associated with maintaining a home. These include shopping, cooking, cleaning, and so forth, but does not include parenting. The homemaker is unpaid and may be a person of either sex. A person who is paid for such work would fit into the Paid Worker Role category.

The following are examples of Homemaker Role-Home Problems:

- A woman who is angry that her roommates do not clean up after themselves.
- A woman who feels that her husband is unwilling to assist her in doing the housework.
- A man who experiences ridicule from friends because he chooses to stay home and do housework and let his wife support the family.
- An elderly widow who lives alone and can no longer shop or cook for herself.

Volunteer. The Volunteer Role assumes some of the responsibilities of the paid worker but the individual is not paid for this work. This role often is performed in health care, community agencies, as well as educational and religious settings. It does not include work performed in professional associations, which would be included under the Member Role.

The following are examples of Volunteer Role Problems:

- A resident of a psychiatric group home who is having trouble performing a volunteer job.
- A volunteer at battered women's shelter agency who is overly involved with the clients and is undermining client self-determination.
- A hospital volunteer who is distressed about the deaths of many of his patients.

Student. A student is someone enrolled in a formal training or educational program. The primary function of the Student Role is acquiring and assimilating knowledge and skills. The following are examples of Student Role Problems:

- A college student who is failing all of his classes
- A woman who has been accepted to medical school, but is unsure whether she can handle the workload.
- A 65-year-old woman who feels out of place returning to the university to complete her education.

Other. Other Occupational Role is used to denote occupational role problems that do not fit into the above roles. In the listing, the worker should specify the type of Other Occupational Role.

The following are examples of Other Occupational Role Problems:

- An athlete who performs poorly and misses the chance to win a medal in her sport and turn professional (Amateur Athlete/Worker Role-Paid Economy)
- A social work student in an agency who is upset because her small stipend has been canceled (Student Role/Volunteer Role)
- A student in a training program who is placed in the same work setting where he is a paid worker and has difficulties dealing with the sometimes conflictual demands of being both a trainee and a regular staff person (Student Role/Worker Role-Paid Economy).

Special Life-Situation Roles

Throughout the course of their lives many people assume time-limited, situation-specific roles in addition to or in place of other possible role.

Consumer. The Consumer Role is assumed by anyone who contracts to receive services or goods from a provider. This role usually includes the exchange of money for goods and services. These providers can include attorneys, real estate agents, or other business people. Excluded from this category are providers of services to treat mental, physical, or psychosocial disorders. These are included under the Patient/Client Roles.

The following are examples of Consumer Role Problems:

- A man who believes his mechanic has not repaired his car as agreed, and the mechanic refuses to refund any money.
- A woman who finds that her real estate agent lied to her by not telling her about major defects in her house.
- A man who finds that his attorney is running up his bill by charging more time than can be accounted for.

Caregiver. The caregiver role is assumed by a person who provides assistance to another in their activities of daily living. The caregiver may be paid or unpaid. It often includes members of the disabled person's family or close friends.

The following are examples of Caregiver Role Problems:

- An 80-year-old man is exhausted trying to care for his wife who suffers from Alzheimer's disease.
- A 75-year old man who can no longer engage in his usual activities because his wife is experiencing severe depression and cannot be left alone.
- A 50-year-old man who has Parkinson's disease and refuses to leave the house requires his wife to spend all her time caring for him.
- The spouse of a disabled man is unable find responsible help in caring for her husband.

Inpatient/Client. The Inpatient/Client Role is assumed by a person who is defined by helping professionals as needing help in an institutional setting, such as in a psychiatric hospital, general hospital, or nursing home.

The following are examples of Inpatient/Client Role Problems:

- A new resident of a halfway house states he does not like living there and wants to move back home.
- An elderly woman becomes verbally assaultive when the staff at her nursing home refuse to call her daughter.
- A seriously ill patient demands to leave the hospital against medical advice.

Outpatient/Client. The Outpatient/Client Role is similar to the Inpatient/Client Role. It is assumed by a person who is defined by helping professionals as being in need of help outside of an institutional setting.

The following are examples of Outpatient/Client Role Problems:

- A woman who is ambivalent about staying with her physician because he prescribes tranquilizers instead of taking the time to assess her problem.
- A suicidal man who refuses his therapist's recommendation for antidepressant medication.
- A young man who does not want to terminate therapy because he has become dependent on his female therapist.

Probationer/Parolee. The Probationer/Parolee Role is assumed by a person who has been convicted of or pled guilty to a criminal charge and who is monitored or supervised by officers of the criminal justice system in lieu of or after serving a sentence.

The following are examples of Probationer/Parolee Role Problems:

- An individual who fails to live up to the conditions of his probation.
- A parolee who served time for a sexual offense cannot return to his hometown because of community outcry.
- A woman who reports that her parole officer has threatened physical violence.

Prisoner. The Prisoner Role is assumed by a person who is incarcerated. The prisoner may be awaiting trial or may have been sentenced for a violation of the law.

The following are examples of Prisoner Role Problems:

- A man convicted of child molestation is worried about being treated harshly by other prisoners.
- A man jailed for a minor offense protests a transfer to a cellblock where there are rival gang members.
- A woman is worried about a new guard transferred to her unit who has a reputation for being cruel.

Legal Immigrant. The Legal Immigrant Role is assumed by a person who has moved from one country to another and is considered legal in the host country. The immigrant may have to deal with the loss of an old way of life, language difficulties, cultural conflict, and hostile reactions from the citizens of the new country.

The following are examples of Legal Immigrant Role Problems:

- A Korean woman married to a white man who is isolated because she is unable to communicate with people in her community.
- A Brazilian man who is ambivalent about staying in the United States because he is worried that his family is losing their traditional values.
- A Russian woman who has never felt comfortable in this country and misses her family.

Undocumented Immigrant. The Undocumented Immigrant Role is similar to the Legal Immigrant Role except that the undocumented immigrant did not immigrate legally and may have to deal with possible apprehension by the authorities.

The following are examples of Undocumented Immigrant Role Problems:

- A pregnant Mexican woman who entered the country illegally five years ago has been told that she will be taken into custody if she has her child in a hospital.
- A man from a Caribbean country has been told that he will not qualify for amnesty under a government program and will be deported.
- A South American man who has family in this country has been caught by the immigration authorities for the third time in a year and is being returned to his country.

Refugee Immigrant. The Refugee Immigrant Role is similar to the Legal Immigrant Role except that the refugee is in flight from his or her native land because of political or religious persecution. The refugee is considered a legal resident of the host country.

The following are examples of Refugee Immigrant Role Problems:

- A Hmong male who recently arrived in the United States believes he will never see his parents again.
- A Muslim woman who divorced her husband is threatened by her in-laws, who say that they will find her and kill her.

Other. Other Special Life-Situation Role should be used to describe roles that are not included in the preceding section.. These are usually time-limited and situation-specific roles that people may experience at different times in their lives. The specific Other Special Life-Situation Role should be noted in the listing.

Types of Role Problems

After identifying the social role area in which the client's problem exists, the next step is to identify the particular type of social role problem the client is experiencing. "Type" is used in the PIE system to describe the kind of interactional difficulty that is occurring or has occurred between the client and another person. This step will help the practitioner conduct a more accurate assessment and intervention plan. For example, the assessment and intervention plan for a client with a Spouse Role Problem who is in conflict with a spouse will differ from that of a client with a Spouse Role Problem resulting from the spouse's death. Similarly, the assessment and intervention plan for a client with a Paid Worker Role Economic Problem who

is in conflict with an employer will be significantly different from that of client with a Paid Worker Role Problem who is being transferred to a less prestigious assignment.

Below is a list of types describing and categorizing commonly observed characteristics or dynamics of social functioning problems. Case examples are provided to illustrate each problem type. It is important to keep in mind that both the social role problem *area* and the social role problem *type* are descriptive of the client's difficulty and not of the other person in the relationship. Although generally both individuals play a role in most interactional difficulties, it is important when typing the problem to focus on the client's presenting problem. Thus, a spouse who is abused might be typed as oppressed/victimization, whereas the abusing spouse's problem might be typed as power conflict. It should be noted that types are not mutually exclusive, and it is possible that a client's type of role problem may include more than one. If this occurs, it is advisable to identify the dominant type. If more than one type is prominent, the mixed-type category can be used.

Type

Power conflict type
Ambivalence type
Obligation/responsibility type
Dependency type
Loss type
Isolation type
Oppressed type
Mixed type
Other type

Power Conflict Type

In its broadest terms, power is the capacity for influence and involves the perceived ability or potential to influence others. Power has also been described as the ability to impose one's will on others, even if others resist in some way. Numerous types and sources of power have been identified. For example, power may be held through delegated authority, knowledge or expertise, control over resources, or through force such as coercion and violence. The social role problem type of Power Conflict most often involves the misuse or abuse of physical or psychological authority and power.

Case Example. A Marine officer is concerned about the rebellious behavior of his adolescent daughter. He perceives her behavior as a personal threat to his authority in his Parent Role. Accustomed to having his orders obeyed, the officer became more coercive when he learned that his daughter had disobeyed him and continued to date a boy he had ordered her to stop seeing. He first threatened the boy and ordered him to stop all communication with his daughter. When his daughter found out about what had occurred she defended her boyfriend. The father became enraged and struck her. Thus, this individual's difficulties in his role of parent could be expressed as Parent Role Problem, Power Conflict type.

The following are examples of other Power Conflict problems:

- A husband who refuses to let his wife work outside the home fearing she will meet another man. (Spouse Role)
- A 40-year-old man with a drug problem who takes advantage of his elderly parents by stealing their money. (Child Role/Adult)
- A supervisor who goes through his employees' desks to see if they are complying with agency policies. (Paid Worker Role)
- A probation officer who tells his parolee that he will overlook a violation if she grants him sexual favors. (Paid Worker Role)

Ambivalence Type

Ambivalence is a state of internal tension involving conflicting feelings about a person or thing. Although the tensions generated by ambivalence have the potential to motivate an individual toward problem solving, they frequently result in feelings of uncertainty, indecisiveness, and vacillation in making a choice. This may result in role performance behaviors that may confuse or sometimes provoke others.

Case Example. A 30-year-old attorney who has been living with her boyfriend for two years is feeling pressured by both her boyfriend and her parents to get married. However, she has mixed feelings about whether this is the right decision, particularly since although she wants to get married, she does not want children. Both her boyfriend and parents, however, think that she is going through a phase and that she will eventually change her mind about this (Lover Role Problem)

The following are other examples of ambivalence problems:

- A college student can't decide between majoring in art, his passion, or business, which is more likely to allow him to make a living (Student Role).
- A prisoner can't decide what to do when he learns about an escape plan that several prisoners are carefully planning. (Prisoner Role).

- A 62-year-old foster parent who has some health problems has an opportunity to adopt a child in her care, but is torn between taking on this responsibility and enjoying her retirement. (Parent Role)

Responsibility Type

A responsibility may be defined as an obligation to perform certain behaviors that one is bound to as a result of a promise, a felt duty, role expectation, or moral necessity. Role performance expectations and sanctions for inadequate performance are defined by a person's community and internalized by the person. Individuals who perform their obligations and responsibilities often experience a sense of well-being and competence from having fulfilled certain role expectations. However, when role expectations or responsibilities are felt to be overwhelming, oppressive, or too difficult, or a person fails to live up to these role expectations, he or she usually experiences strain and distress.

Case Example. A young mother in a lesbian relationship reports that she is frustrated and feels that she is failing as a parent because she does not know how to help her nine-year-old son cope with bullying at school. She reports that he come homes in tears because other children make fun of him for having two mothers. This woman's problem would be coded as Parent Role Problem, Responsibility type.

The following are other examples of Responsibility type problems:

- A new officer in a community organization wants to resign because he feels unable to meet his new responsibilities. (Member Role)
- An unemployed father of a new born is anxious and depressed because he is unable to meet the responsibilities of supporting another child. (Parent Role)
- A social worker at a Child Protection Service agency has such a large caseload that she feels unable to provide quality care to her clients unless she puts in 10 hours of overtime per week, for which she does not get paid. (Paid Worker Role-Economic Problem)
- A student comes to the counseling office reporting he is unable to keep up with the course work. (Student Role)

Dependency Type

No one is totally independent. We are all dependent on each other in some way. Children rely on parents, elderly and sick individuals rely on caregivers and spouses/partners rely on each other for meeting a variety of emotional, sexual, companionship, and financial needs. Healthy individuals are aware that even as they strive to be independent, they are also ultimately dependent on others around them, on their society and ecosystem.

Dependency may become a problem when there is a pervasive or excessive need to be taken care of or a denial of normal dependency needs. Adults with dependency problems often exhibit submissive and clinging behaviors and perceive themselves as being unable to function adequately without the help of others. Alternatively, adults with dependency problems may refuse to recognize any need for help or reliance on others. It is important to note, however, that culture influences role performance expectations with respect to independent behavior, as well as how dependency needs are net.

Case Example. A 56-year-old man is married to a woman who manages all aspect of their lives. She was the only person he ever dated and he met her through his sister. He has been employed in his father's business since graduation from high school. In his social relationships he clings to others and never initiates plans. He expects others to make arrangement for all social and professional activities and looks to others to offer advice and fix any problem that arises. (Spouse Role).

The following are other examples of Dependency type problems:

- A woman is unable to go out of her house without the assistance of her best friend (Friend Role).
- A woman defers all decisions about her health care to her physician (Outpatient/Client Role).
- A 33-year-old male is unemployed, living at home, and financially dependent on his parents (Child Role).

Loss Type

Loss is a part of everyone's life. How an individual responds to a loss or separation is influenced not just by the event itself, but also by a multitude of different factors. Such things as the nature of the attachment to the lost person or object, the circumstances of the loss (for example, was it unexpected, the result of violence, or the culmination of a long illness), previous experiences with loss, availability of caring social supports, an individual's coping style, and cultural and religious beliefs all influence how a person responds.

Significant separations or losses such as the death of a loved one; a divorce; the loss of home, job, or personal relationship; a move; or a decline in health often evoke anxiety with accompanying intense feelings of loss, anger, depression, loneliness, fear, hopelessness, or guilt.

Social role performance under these circumstances can become difficult. For many people, the loss of a role is in itself a highly significant life event. The loss may bring a sudden and unsettling change in life's basic circumstances. There may be a marked decline in financial means, having to live alone, or not being able to continue to live in a familiar setting.

Case Example. A 30-year-old man was referred by his physician for severe depression following the loss of his wife in an automobile accident. (Spouse Role).

The following are other examples of Loss type problems:

- After 20 years of marriage a husband learns that his wife wants to end the marriage. (Spouse Role)
- A 65-year-old man reports that his wife who suffers from Alzheimer's disease no longer recognizes him. (Spouse Role)
- A 38-year-old woman who had become pregnant through in vitro fertilization has a miscarriage in her seventh month of pregnancy. (Parent Role)
- An undocumented immigrant who has a family and a successful roofing business is apprehended and placed in detention. (Undocumented Immigrant Role)

Isolation Type

Isolation means being disconnected or separate from others. Individuals who withdraw or isolate themselves from others do so for varied reasons. For some it may be response to a perceived hurt. For example, the loss or hurt in an important relationship may cause a person to withdraw from that relationship and possibly others. Those who are fearful or uncomfortable in their social relationships or prescribed social roles may withdraw and isolate themselves from what they perceive as the stress of participation. Others may isolate from others because of an emotional, behavioral, or serious mental health problem such as agoraphobia. Some may withdraw or isolate themselves due to problems stemming from medical conditions. For example, an elderly woman may socially withdraw because she is embarrassed by her incontinence. An individual with AIDS may withdraw from friends and family because she or he fears ostracism. People in new situations or communities may have problems establishing new relationships and the social roles familiar to them may not be adaptive. For some, social isolation may be a chronic state related to long-standing problems related to low elf-esteem, insecurity, or a mental disorder.

Case Example. A 38-year-old single woman has always been very shy. Over the past eight years she has gained more than 70 pounds. Although she desires friend-ships, she has become more isolated from others. She reports being embarrassed about her appearance and fear-ful about how others would respond if they really knew her. This woman's problem could be coded as Friend Role Problem, Isolation type.

The following are other examples of Isolation type problems:

- A man in a nursing home no longer wishes to com-municate with the other patients. (Inpatient/Client Role)
- A young woman who learns she is HIV positive refuses to see her old friends and acquaintances. (Friend Role)
- A soldier returning from Iraq moves to an isolated cabin because he can no longer tolerate being around other people. (Other Special Life Situation Role, Veteran)

Oppressed Type

Oppression and victimization are the result of exploitation and the unjust use of force or authority. Relationships involving physical or psychological abuse of power that result in a person feeling kept down, intimidated, fearful, or exploited often over a lengthy period of time character-ize the Oppressed type of role functioning problem. Victims often experience a range of symptoms including numbing, fear, anxiety, distress, anger, self-blame, alien-ation, powerlessness, and fear of future harm.

Case Example. A 29-year-old Cambodian woman came to a local agency that serves the Asian community. She reported that she and her husband were married in Cambodia and came to the United States four years ago. Approximately six months ago, her husband lost his job and since that time problems in the marriage escalated. She reported that her husband had become more argu-mentative, controlling and demanding, especially sexu-ally. During the past week, he beat her when she would not comply sexually. This woman's role problem may be coded as Spousal Role, Oppressed type.

The following are other examples of Oppressed-type problems:

- An elderly man's drug-addicted son is draining his meager financial resources. (Parent Role)
- A woman is raped by her dating partner. (Lover Role)
- A member of a religious group has been threatened with excommunication if he speaks out against the group's financial mismanagement. (Member Role)
- An undocumented immigrant tolerates terrible working conditions. (Undocumented Immigrant Role)

Mixed Type

The mixed type should be used when no one dimension of role performance is predominant and when the role prob-lem can best be described by a mixture of dimensions. The mixed category should be used sparingly. Whenever pos-sible a predominant type should determined and used.

The following are examples of Mixed type problems:

- A father loses a child and withdraws from his other children. (Parent Role, Loss type and Isolation type)
- A student is ambivalent about graduating withdraws from her studies and her friends. (Student Role, Ambivalence type and Isolation type)
- A mother of a child diagnosed with a rare and termi-nal form of cancer is ambivalent regarding whether to have her child undergo another aggressive round of chemotherapy and radiation or take her home and enjoy the last few months of her life. (Parent Role, Loss type and Ambivalence type)

Other Type

The other type should be used when none of the listed dimensions of role performance adequately describe the case dynamics.

CHAPTER 4

Factor II: Person in Environment—Problems in The Environment

In the social role problems previously listed, attention has been given to interpersonal transactions that affect social functioning. The environmental problems that follow are the factors outside of the client, located in the community or larger social environment, that affect social functioning and well-being. The environment provides both resources and opportunities.

Listed below are six systems located in one's community/larger environment that when operating effectively create a climate of social well-being for its members. (Refer to Chapter 1 of Person-In-Environment (Karls & Wandrei, 1994) for how this system was developed). It is important to identify problems in those systems, because they impinge on the social functioning problems. By locating a problem in the social system and environment, the practitioner can make a considered decision about whether to intervene in the interpersonal problem, the environmental problem, or both.

Those six subsystems are as follows:

1. *Basic Needs System.* The system of social institutions and social agencies that provides food, shelter, employment, funds, and transportation.
2. *Education and Training System.* The system of social institutions that transmits knowledge and skills, educates people about the values of the society, and serves in the development of skills that are needed to maintain the society.
3. *Judicial and Legal System:* The system of social institutions and social agencies that controls the social behavior of people.
4. *Health, Safety, and Social Services System.* The system of social institutions and social agencies that provides for health (including mental health), safety, and social services.

5. *Voluntary Association System.* The system of religious organizations and community social support groups that facilitates social and spiritual growth and development.
6. *Affectional Support System.* The system of friendships and acquaintances that constitutes a person's individual social support system.

For each of the six Environmental Systems identified, a number of specific problems areas are listed

Environmental Systems

(1) Basic Needs System Problem Areas:
Food/Nutrition
Shelter
Employment
Economic Resources
Transportation
Discrimination
(2) Education and Training System Problem Areas
Education and Training
Discrimination
(3) Judicial and Legal System Problem Areas
Justice and Legal
Discrimination
(4) Health, Safety, and Social Services System Problem Areas
Health/Mental Health
Safety
Social Services
Discrimination
(5) Voluntary Association System Problem Areas
Religious Groups

Community Groups
Discrimination
(6) Affectional Support System Problem Areas
Affectional Support
Discrimination

Definitions of System Problems

Basic Needs System

The problems in the Basic Needs System category are those related to the production, distribution, and consumption functions of the society's economic system. Problems in this category consist of those related to meeting basic needs for food, shelter, and clothing as well as acquiring goods and services.

Food/Nutrition

- Lack of food supply on a regular basis (for example, a drought).
- Food supply inadequate for nutrition with potential threat to health (for example, no fresh vegetables or fruits).
- Inadequate water supply, with threat to health (for example, only powdered infant formula available in a community with poor water system).
- Other food/nutrition problem (specify) (for example, a food supply exists, but civil war prevents delivery).

Shelter

- Absence of shelter in a community on a regular basis (for example, no housing for poor people or those with low incomes).
- Inadequate or substandard housing in a community (for example, housing not meeting building and health codes).
- Other shelter problem (specify) (for example, shelter for homeless people available only during the winter months).

Employment

- No work available in the community.
- Insufficient employment (for example, only part-time or low-wage jobs available in the community).
- Inappropriate employment (lack of socially and legally acceptable employment in the community, for example, dealing drugs is the only source of income available in the community).
- Other employment problem (specify) (for example, only dangerous employment in an unsafe chemical plant available).

Economic Resources

- Insufficient resources for basic sustenance in community (for example, public assistance inadequate to meet basic needs).
- Insufficient resources in community to provide for needed services beyond sustenance (for example, no public assistance for other necessary items, such as wheelchairs and child care).
- Regulatory barriers to economic resources (for example, overly restrictive regulations for eligibility for general assistance).
- Other economic resources problem (specify) (for example, public assistance checks delayed or lost).

Transportation

- No transportation for accessibility to job, special services, or social services (for example, there is no public transportation system in the community).
- Inadequate transportation for client access to job, special services, or social services (for example, there is inadequate public transportation system in the community).
- Other transportation problem (for example, the public transportation system does not run at night).

Discrimination

- Age discrimination (for example, mandatory retirement age of 65).
- Ethnicity, color, or language discrimination (for example, African Americans not promoted in a fire department)
- Religious discrimination (for example, Orthodox Jews required to work on Saturdays).
- Gender discrimination (for example, men promoted rather than qualified women).
- Sexual orientation discrimination (for example, gay men and lesbians denied entry into the military).
- Lifestyle discrimination (for example, landlords not renting to communes).
- Noncitizen status discrimination (for example, landlords not renting to undocumented workers).

- Veteran status discrimination (for example, an employer biased against veterans).
- Dependency status discrimination (for example, landlords not renting to people on welfare).
- Disability discrimination (for example, no wheelchair lifts on public buses).
- Marital status discrimination (for example, married women not given partnerships in law firms).
- Body size (for example, an obese woman refused transport to a medical clinic.
- Political affiliation (for example, the owner of a restaurant refusing to serve a group of protestors against the war in Iraq.)
- Other discrimination in Basic Needs System (specify) (for example, landlords not renting to parents with young children).

Education and Training System Problems

The problems in this category refer to the existence, efficiency and accessibility of schools and institutions.

Education and Training

- Lack of educational or training facilities (for example, no vocational training programs).
- Lack of relevant, adequate or appropriate facilities (for example, no programs for adults who want to earn high school diplomas).
- Lack of culturally relevant educational or training opportunities (for example, no vocational training programs for monolingual Hmong-speaking people).
- Regulatory barriers to existing educational and training services and programs (for example, overly restrictive requirements to qualify for vocational training programs).
- Absence of support services needed to gain access to educational/training opportunities (for example, no child care at a vocational college).
- Other Education and Training System problem (specify) (for example, a college library not open on the weekend).

Discrimination

- Age discrimination (for example, people older than 50 not allowed to enter a training program).
- Ethnicity, color, or language discrimination (for example, Asians harassed at the police academy).
- Religious discrimination (for example, examinations scheduled on Jewish New Year).

- Sex discrimination (for example, different dormitory curfew hours for female students).
- Sexual orientation discrimination (for example, gay men and lesbians not allowed to enter the police academy).
- Lifestyle discrimination (for example, children of commune members harassed at school).
- Noncitizen status discrimination (for example, a training program requiring U.S. citizenship).
- Veteran status discrimination (for example, military training not accepted as equivalent to vocational training).
- Dependency status discrimination (for example, welfare clients not accepted into a car repair training course).
- Disability discrimination (for example, a college not providing readers for blind students).
- Marital status discrimination (for example, a hospital not accepting married women for medical residencies).
- Body size discrimination (for example, obese children refused soft drinks at school)
- Political affiliation (for example, a liberal student refused admission to a religious conservative school.
- Other Education and Training System discrimination (specify) (for example, social workers not accepted into a psychoanalytic training institute).

Judicial and Legal System Problems

The problems in this category refer to those involving the criminal justice system, which include police department, courts, prisons, jails, and probation and parolee services. These are institutions designed to protect society.

Judicial and Legal

- Lack of police services (for example, no police station in a small town).
- Lack of relevant police services (for example, no sexual assault specialist).
- Lack of confidence in police services (for example, police viewed as slow to respond to domestic violence calls).
- Lack of adequate prosecution or defense services (for example, not enough public defenders to handle the caseload).
- Lack of adequate probation or parole services (for example, no work furlough program).
- Other Judicial and Legal System problem (specify) (for example, judges inadequately trained to handle child abuse cases).

Discrimination

- Age discrimination (for example, no programs for older offenders).
- Ethnicity, color, or language discrimination (for example, African Americans harassed by the police).
- Religious discrimination (for example, Sikhs not allowed to become police officers).
- Sex discrimination (for example, no halfway houses for female offenders).
- Sexual orientation discrimination (for example, homophobic judges).
- Lifestyle discrimination (for example, homeless people are harassed by police).
- Noncitizen status discrimination (for example, public defenders not defending noncitizens).
- Veteran status discrimination (for example, Gulf war veterans with PTSD sentenced to jail rather than provided with psychiatric treatment).
- Dependency status discrimination (for example, welfare parents more likely to have children taken away).
- Disability discrimination (for example, deaf people cannot serve on juries).
- Marital status discrimination (for example, only legally married prisoners have conjugal visits).
- Body size discrimination (for example, no individualized sleeping accommodations for incarcerated obese individuals).
- Political Affiliation, (for example, political protestors put down by the. police).
- Other Judicial and Legal System discrimination (for example, police not arresting other police officers who commit crimes).

Health, Safety, and Social Services System Problems

The problems in this category refer to those involving systems that provide health, mental health, public safety and social services to those in need. The focus in this category is not on the health or other problems of the individual but on the existence and availability of services that sustain the health and welfare of the individual.

Health/Mental Health

- Absence of adequate health services (for example, no AIDS testing available).
- Regulatory barriers to health services (for example, Medicare not covering a needed health service).

- Inaccessibility of health services (for example, closest dialysis center 100 miles away).
- Absence of support services needed to use health services (for example, no child care available during clinic hours).
- Absence of adequate mental health services (for example, no day treatment available).
- Regulatory barriers to mental health services (for example, client not meeting residency criteria to receive outpatient services).
- Inaccessibility of mental health services (for example, the community mental health clinic 100 miles away).
- Absence of support services needed to use mental health services (for example, no translator for case management services available).
- Other health/mental health services system problem (specify) (for example, employer termination of health insurance because of excessive cost).

Safety

- Violence or crime in neighborhood (for example, a client living next to a meth house).
- Unsafe working conditions (for example, a client working with toxic chemicals).
- Unsafe conditions in home (for example, a house not meeting earthquake standards).
- Absence of adequate safety services (for example, no fire department in a rural area).
- Natural disaster of large proportions (for example, a major flood).
- Human-created disaster (for example, a refinery explosion).

stop signs at a busy intersection).

Social Services

Absence of adequate social services (for example, no homeless programs).

Regulatory barriers to social services (for example, a means test).

Inaccessibility of social services (for example, a hot line for parents not open on the weekend).

Absence of support services needed to use social services (for example, no case management provided to a client in a parent education class).

Other social services problem (specify) (for example, inability of a client to meet with a social worker because of the worker's huge caseload).

Discrimination

Age discrimination (for example, an adoption agency not placing children with older adults).

Ethnicity, color, or language discrimination (for example, no mental health services available in Spanish).

Religious discrimination (for example, a hospital not providing culturally competent services for Muslim patients).

Sex discrimination (for example, a residential treatment program that excludes females).

Sexual orientation discrimination (for example, a hospital not allowing the partner of a gay man spousal visitation rights).

Lifestyle discrimination (for example, smokers refused health insurance).

Noncitizen status discrimination (for example, requiring proof of citizenship to obtain social services).

Veteran status discrimination (for example, veterans denied services because they are expected to obtain services through the Veterans Administration)

Dependency status (for example, physicians not accepting Medicaid reimbursement)

Disability discrimination (for example, an agency without wheelchair ramps).

Marital status discrimination (for example, a religious social services agency not providing services to divorced clients).

Body size discrimination (for example, an obese male denied food stamps)

Political discrimination (for example, a mental health practitioner refusing to provide services to people affiliated with an extremist political party).

Other Health, Safe and Social Services System discrimination (specify) (for example, a health clinic not serving a person who is a meth addict).

Voluntary Association System Problems

The problems in this category refer to those involving organized or informal religious and community groups. Religious groups are defined as those formally organized around a belief system pertaining to an ultimate reality or deity and having a commitment to religious faith or observance. Community groups are composed of people with common interests or characteristics banded together for social exchange and support. Among these are social clubs and self-help organizations.

Religious Groups

Lack of religious group of choice (for example, no Catholic parish in a rural area).

Lack of community acceptance of religious values (for example, community harassment of Muslims).

Other religious group problem (specify) (for example, a religious group trying to recruit people who are not interested in being recruited).

Community Groups

• Lack of community support group of choice (for example, no AA groups).

• Lack of community acceptance of community group of choice (for example, members of a fraternity refused service in a community).

• Other community group problem (specify) (for example, community groups fight with one another).

Discrimination

Age discrimination (for example, a church not having a group for seniors).

Ethnicity color, or language discrimination (for example, a religious denomination not allowing for services in Hmong).

Religious discrimination (for example, nuns are accepted as leaders of a community organization).

Sex discrimination (for example, women not accepted as clergy).

Sexual orientation discrimination (for example, a religious denomination not accepting gay or lesbian or transgender individuals).

Lifestyle discrimination (for example, vegan parents refused membership on a school board).

Noncitizen status discrimination (for example, a community group requireing citizenship status for membership).

Veteran status discrimination (for example, veterans not accepted as members of an anti-war group).

Dependency status discrimination (for example, women on welfare not accepted by a single-parent group).

Disability discrimination (for example, people with developmental delays not allowed into a church group).

Marital status discrimination (for example, single parents not allowed to join a parent cooperative).

Body size discrimination (for example, an athletic club's refusal to accept a dwarf).

Political discrimination (for example, a Democratic club refusing to accept a Republican).

Other Voluntary Association System discrimination (specify) (for example, police officers not accepted into a peace group).

Affectional Support System Problems

The problems in this category refer to those involving the network of social relationships in an individual's social support system. This system can consist of nuclear family, extended family, family of origin, friends, acquaintances, coworkers, paid or volunteer helpers, and service providers such as bartenders, beauticians, postal employees and police officers. The Affectional Support System includes everyone who has an affectional tie with the client.

Affectional Support

- Absence of an affectional support system (for example, no friends, relatives, or acquaintances available to a client).
- Support system is inadequate to meet affectional needs of client (for example, friends, relatives, and acquaintances exist, who are not able to provide emotional support to the client).
- Excessively involved support system (for example, an overprotective family not allowing a disabled person to live independently).
- Other Affectional Support System problem (specify) (for example, a client's Affectional Support System mostly composed of substance abusers).

Discrimination

- Age discrimination (for example, older members of the family excluded from family events).

- Ethnicity, color, or language discrimination (for example, a support system not accepting a client's spouse who is of a different race).
- Religious discrimination (for example, family rejection of a client who married outside of the family's religion).
- Sex discrimination (for example, a client's support system insisting that a man needs less support than a woman).
- Sexual orientation discrimination (for example, a client's support system shuns any transgender person).
- Lifestyle discrimination (for example, a client's support system shunning a woman who smokes).
- Noncitizen status discrimination (for example, coworkers rejecting a man when they find out he is not a citizen).
- Veteran status discrimination (for example, a politically radical family refusing to provide housing for a son returning from fighting in an unpopular war).
- Dependency status discrimination (for example, family members withdrawing when a woman goes on welfare).
- Disability discrimination (for example, a client's support system withdrawing after he develops Parkinson's disease).
- Marital status discrimination (for example, the support system rejecting a recent widow).
- Body size discrimination (for example, a member of the family constantly being teased because she is too thin by their standards).
- Political discrimination (for example, a group of friends refusing to accept a person who switches political parties).
- Other Affectional Support System discrimination (specify) (for example, a woman rejected by childless friends after she has a baby).

CHAPTER 5

Factor III: Mental Health Condition and Factor IV: Physical Health Conditions

Factor III: Mental Health Conditions

In the PIE system it is important to have as clear a picture as possible of the client's mental health condition. Factor III identifies any mental health problems the client is experiencing. The practitioner licensed to diagnose mental health disorders most often uses Axis I and Axis II of the DSM (*Diagnostic and Statistical Manual*) of the American Psychiatric Association (2000). Some practitioners may use the ICD-10 or the ICF. In cases where the practitioner is not licensed to diagnose, the diagnosis of a licensed practitioner should be used, if available. In some cases the client might report a mental disorder, which should be noted. For practitioners using the DSM, Axis I and Axis II consist of the following:

- Axis I: Clinical disorders, including major mental disorders, as well as developmental and learning disorders
- Axis II: Personality disorders and mental retardation.

In addition to recording the psychiatric diagnoses, the severity and duration of the condition are noted as well as the client's coping ability and any mental health strengths. Recording the severity and duration of problems and clients' coping capacities and strengths are discussed more fully in the next chapter.

Factor IV: Physical Health Conditions

In the PIE system it is important to have a clear understanding of the client's physical health condition. Factor IV identifies any current physical disorder or condition that is potentially relevant to the understanding the social role functioning of a client. Practitioners may use either Axis III of the DSM, the ICD–10 or the ICF. Because many practitioners are not licensed to make physical diagnoses, the source of the diagnosis should be noted. For example, the worker might note on Factor IV "Diabetes (by report of the client)," or "Cirrhosis of liver (diagnosed by Dr. X)," or "Client reports no physical problems."

In some instances, a client's physical condition may be an important source of social role or environmental problems (for example, Chronic Fatigue syndrome in a client with a Spousal Role problem, Responsibility type or AIDS in a client with a Lover Role Problem, Loss type). In another instance the physical disorder may not be the source of the client's problems, but it may be important in planning an overall intervention strategy (for example, obesity in a person with a Paid Worker Role Problem, Loss type). The practitioner may just wish to note significant associated physical findings (for example, asthma in a client with a Client/Inpatient Role Problem).

Severity, Duration, Coping, and Strengths Indexes

In the PIE system, it is important to know the severity of the problem, its duration and the ability of the client to cope with the problem. In addition, it is important to know the strengths and resources available that can be used when working with the client. The Severity Index indicates the degree of disruption or stress experienced by the client. The Duration Index measures the recency and duration of the problem. The Coping Index estimates the internal resources available to the client for addressing the identified problems. The Strength Index directs practitioners to acknowledge and appreciate client's capacities as well as to identify community resources or assets. The practitioner should use all four indexes to complete the description of the client's social functioning and environmental problems and to provide an indication of whether intervention is required.

Severity Index

The Severity Index is used on all factors. The index has a five-point scale with 1 or L (Low) as the lowest and 5 or C (Catastrophic) as the highest degree of severity.

The five levels of the Severity Index are:

1	Low	L
2	Moderate	M
3	High	H
4	Very high	H+
5	Catastrophic	C

Low severity = 1 or L

The problem may include some change but is perceived as nondisruptive by the client, although some disruption may be noted by the practitioner. Intervention may be desirable but not necessary. Examples include starting school, getting a traffic ticket, or having an argument with a neighbor.

Moderate severity = 2 or M

The problem is disruptive to the client's functioning, but the distress is not judged as impairing general functioning. Intervention would be helpful. Examples include separating from a spouse or partner, losing a job, having the last child leave home.

High severity = 3 or H

The problem is characterized by changes in key or multiple areas of social role functioning or in the environment. Early intervention is indicated. Examples include getting a divorce, major financial loss, or the death of a friend.

Very high severity = 4 or H+

The problem involves more dramatic changes, and the client is in a clear state of distress. Immediate intervention is probably necessary. Examples include the death of a spouse or partner, serious illness, or rape.

Catastrophic = 5 or C

The problem is characterized by sudden, negative changes with devastating implications for adjustment. Immediate direct intervention is indicated. Problems of this severity are induced by events such as torture, multiple family deaths, and loss of loved ones and possessions in a natural disaster.

Duration Index

The Duration Index is used on all four factors and indicates the length or recency of the problem. The Duration Index rating ranges from 1 or Y: 5+ = more than five years, to

5 or W:1–4 = one to four weeks, with the higher number generally indicating great urgency of intervention.

The five levels of the Duration Index and their codes are:

1	5 or more years	Y: 5+
2	1–5 years	Y: 1–5
3	6–12 months	M: 6–12
4	1–6 months	M: 1–6
5	1–4 weeks	W: 1–4

Coping Index

The Coping Index is a measure or rating of the client's ability to manage a problem given his or her internal resources. Using best clinical skills, the practitioner rates the client's ability to solve problems and to act independently. The Coping Index ratings range from Outstanding, coded as 1 or A, to Inadequate, coded as 5 or F. If the practitioner is unable to make a judgment, record as 6 or I = Unable to judge at this time. The six levels of the Coping Index are:

1	Outstanding	A
2	Above average	B
3	Adequate	C
4	Somewhat inadequate	D
5	Inadequate	F
6	Unable to judge at this time	I

Outstanding coping skills = 1 or A
The client's ability to solve problems, act independently, and to use ego strength, insight, and intellectual ability to cope with difficult situations is exceptional.

Above-average coping skills = 2 or B
The client's ability to solve problems, act independently, and to use ego strength, insight, and intellectual ability to cope with difficult situations is more than would be expected in the average person.

Adequate coping skills = 3 or C
The client is able to solve problems, act independently, and has adequate ego strength, insight, and intellectual ability.

Somewhat inadequate coping skills = 4 or D
The client has fair problem-solving ability but has major difficulties solving the presenting problems, acting independently, and using ego strength, insight, or intellectual ability.

Inadequate coping skills = 5 or E
The client shows little or no ability to solve problems, lacks the capacity to act independently, and has insufficient ego strength, insight, and intellectual ability.

No coping skills = 6 or I
The practitioner is unable to judge client's coping ability at this time.

The Strength Index

The PIE system uses the strengths perspective as a way of identifying positive elements in the client's life situation. Highlighting strengths and resilience permits the practitioner to develop a more positive working relationship and can be used as a starting point to create hope and a positive vision for change. The Strengths Index is used to indicate positive Social Role and Relationship Functioning (Factor I), Environmental situations (Factor II), Mental Heath Conditions (Factor III) and Physical Health Conditions (Factor IV). In the PIE system, there are two kinds of strengths, Notable =1 or N and Possible = 2 or P. These are defined as follows:

Notable strengths = 1 or N
Notable strengths refer to those that are more clearly identifiable and accessible and that can be activated for planning and intervention.

Possible strengths = 2 or P
Possible strengths are those that are less easily identifiable or accessible or may need further exploration to determine whether they can be utilized as part of treatment planning.

7 CHAPTER

Intervention Plan

As illustrated in the preceding chapters, the PIE system provides an orderly and multifaceted assessment of the person–in–environment configuration. The PIE system helps the practitioner to understand the multiple factors contributing to the client's difficulties as well as the individual's strengths and community/environmental assets. The helping process has often been conceptualized as comprising three distinct phases:

(1) engagement, assessment and planning,
(2) the change oriented phase and
(3) termination. Each of these phases requires considerable knowledge, skill, and competence on the practitioner's part.

Assessment is one of the most important processes in social work practice because treatment planning and interventions are largely based on the problems and strengths identified in the assessment. Treatment planning and interventions should be directed to those systems that play the most significant role in contributing to clients' problem and should be appropriate for those systems. Treatment planning involves an exploration of the client's desired goals or outcomes and the ways and means to reach these goals. The stated goals should be clear and realistic. Sometimes clients are overwhelmed by the severity or complexity of their problems. Particularly in these situations, setting goals can provide direction and also enhance client's sense of hopefulness.

It is important that client and worker mutually determine the goals of treatment. Thus, after an agreement is reached regarding the nature of the problems and the systems involved, both the client and worker need to come to an agreement on intervention goals and objectives and formulate a plan to achieve those ends. Mutuality in setting goals not only supports clients' self-determination but also is consonant with an empowerment perspective.

Regardless of their theoretical orientation, practitioners generally agree on the goals of treatment, however, they often differ on how to reach the goals, that is, they may differ on what specific intervention strategies will most effectively accomplish the goal. PIE provides a structure within which the practitioner can define goals and interventions clearly. Yet, just as important, PIE allows its users full latitude in deciding what theoretical frameworks and interventions to use. Also, because it might not be possible to address all client problems, the practitioner should designate which interventions should have priority by identifying the intervention as a low, medium or high priority. For each problem identified PIE provides a section for the user to address:

(1) What is the goal of the intervention?
(2) What is the recommended intervention?
(3) What is the priority of the intervention?
(4) Who is to work with the client? (Referral)
(5) What is the expected outcome?

List of Interventions

The following is a list of common interventions that can be used for treatment planning once a PIE assessment is completed. The interventions are arbitrarily divided into three groups: one that targets the interpersonal problems usually found in Factor I; one that targets environmental problems usually found in Factor II; and one that targets intrapersonal problems usually found in Factor III. The terms used to describe the interventions are taken from social work literature and are not defined. The practitioner may wish to utilize the Social Work Dictionary (Barker, 2003) or the

Encyclopedia of Social Work (Edwards, 1995) or do a computer search to obtain definitions and descriptions of the interventions. Some of the terms overlap; they repeat other listings and could be listed in several different categories. Some terms are derived from treatment theories and some reflect techniques used in these treatment theories. This list is not exhaustive. There are other interventions that could be added.

Interventions Focused on the Individual—Targeting Factors I and Factor III

Art Therapy
Assertiveness training
Anger management
Bibliotherapy
Behavior therapy
Career counseling
Cognitive therapy
Cognitive restructuring
Crisis Intervention
EMDR (Eye Movement Desensitization
    Reprocessing)
Existential therapy
Expressive therapies
Empowerment approach
Feminist therapy
Gestalt therapy
Guided imagery
Genetic counseling
Grief work
Hypnotherapy
Imagery relaxation therapy
Implosive therapy
Individual psychotherapy (e.g., Adlerian,
    Attachment, Ego psychology, Jungian,
    Humanistic, Person-centered, etc.)
Inpatient treatment/hospitalization
Journal writing
Mindfulness/ Focusing
Modeling and role-playing
Narrative therapy
Problem solving approach
Psychoanalysis
Psychodynamic
Psychotropic medications
Paradoxical intention
Rational emotive therapy
Reality therapy
Residential treatment

Sex education/Sex therapy
Solution focused
Spiritual counseling
Systematic sensitization
Stress management
Transactional analysis
Task centered approach/Task assignment
Vocational guidance
Vocational rehabilitation

Interventions Focused on Families and Groups Targeting Factor I or Factor III

Communication training
Conjoint therapy
Couples/marital treatment
Divorce therapy
Family treatment/family therapy
    Family life education
    Behavioral family therapy
    Bowenian
    Experiential family therapy
    Strategic family therapy
    Structural family therapy
    Narrative family therapy
    Social Constructionism family therapy
    Brief family therapy
    Feminist family therapy
    Solution focused
Foster care (adult and child)
Group work
    Self help
    Support group
    Psychodynamic group
    Interpersonal group treatment
Mediation
Milieu therapy
Multiple impact therapy
Network therapy
Parent training
Psychodrama
Sibling therapy
Social skills training

Interventions Targeting Environmental Problems—Factor II

Active resistance
Bargaining

Boycott
Case advocacy
Client advocacy
Community organizing
Confrontation
Consultation
Cooptation
Day care
Developing therapeutic milieu
Community education
Forming alliances

Interpretation to community
  or influential
Mediation
Negotiation
Networking
Ombudsperson intervention
Passive resistance
Placement facilitation
Political action
Use of influentials
Use of mass media

Instructions For Recording Case Findings Using CompuPIE and the PIE Worksheet

Identifying, categorizing, and recording problems presented by clients are critical steps in providing effective service delivery. The PIE system enables social workers and other the human services practitioners to identify and sort out the complex array of problems and environmental constraints clients present. Recording these findings can be a tedious but necessary task. The recording tools presented here are designed to help practitioners cover all the PIE Factors and to produce a succinct assessment of the client's situation. Along with the summary of findings are recommendations for interventions that might resolve or reduce the issues that brought the client to the practitioner for help.

To facilitate recording there are two tools included with this manual: the CompuPIE software and the PIE Worksheet

CompuPIE software records findings electronically whereas the PIE Worksheet is used for manual recording of findings. Both tools are intended to be guides for recording assessment findings and developing intervention plans. Unlike CompuPIE, The PIE Worksheet is not copyrighted and so may be reproduced for use by practitioners, teachers, students, and researchers. For instructions on installing the CompuPIE software, refer to Appendix 1.

Instructions for Recording Case Findings

The following set of instructions is intended to accompany the CompuPIE software program and the PIE Worksheet. These instructions presume the practitioner has knowledge of the terms used in the PIE System and is familiar with the PIE concepts and structure. Both the CompuPIE software and the Worksheet may be adapted to accommodate existing recording systems.

In practice most practitioners complete the problem assessment first and then identify client and environment strengths. Recommendations for interventions are usually made after the four Factors in the assessment have been completed and the assessment findings have been summarized

Recording Factor I: Social Role and Relationship Functioning Problem

In Factor I there are four larger categories of social roles with 26 specific roles in which problems can be identified. The four categories are:

(1) Familial,
(2) Other Interpersonal,
(3) Occupational, and
(4) Special Life Situation. The specific roles include spouse, parent, neighbor, student, inpatient worker, and so forth. Refer to chapter 3 for a complete list, descriptions, and definitions. Factor I assessment also includes the severity and duration of the problem. Practitioners using the strengths perspective should include the client's ability to cope and any special client strengths.

The **PIE Worksheet** displays the categories and social roles. It provides tables and indexes to assist in choosing and writing in appropriate descriptions. Acronyms or numbers can be used for easier manual recording. See the Worksheet for a list of acronyms used in the PIE System. The CompuPIE software provides pull-down menus for selecting appropriate categories, roles, and problem descriptions.

Follow the steps below to record Factor I findings.

Step I: Identify Social Role and Relationship Problems, Problem Type, Severity, and Duration

1. Record <u>all</u> the **Social Role and Relationship functioning** problems that the practitioner and client identify. For example, a marital problem would be identified as a Spouse Role Problem. A problem with an employer would be identified as a Paid Worker Problem. It is not uncommon to have more than one problem. It is also possible to have more than one problem in the same role. The PIE system allows you to enter as many different problems as are identified for each client/patient.

2. Record the **Relationship type** linked to each social relationship role. To do so, you may need to refer to the relationship types described in chapter 3 although some terms are self-explanatory. For example, a person losing a spouse by death or divorce is identified as having a Spouse Role, Loss Type Problem. If you identify two or more relationship types in one social role, use the Mixed category and describe in detail in the Case History, Dynamics, and Comments section. If you have insufficient information to make a choice, use the Undetermined category and note this in the Comments section.

3. Record the **severity** of each problem on a five-point scale using the Severity Index. The degree of severity is a clinical judgment that ideally should be made with the client's concurrence. Users of the PIE Worksheet may use the abbreviations to simplify recording. A higher level of severity indicates a greater severity and generally a higher priority for intervention.

4. Record the **duration** of each problem on a five-point scale using the Duration Index. The Duration Index ranges from recent [4 weeks or less] to chronic [5 years or over]. In the PIE System recent onset generally indicates a higher level of priority for intervention.

Step II: Identify Strengths

1. Record your estimate of the **ability of the client to cope** with each problem using the five-point scale in the Coping Index. The Coping Index ranges from " no coping skills" to "outstanding".

2. Record all the **social role and relationship functioning strengths** that the practitioner and the client identify. For example, having a supportive friend would be identified as Friend Role strength. Multiple strengths are common. The practitioner should note the existence of the strength on the worksheet and may elaborate in the Comments Section of the Summary. There is a pull down menu in the CompuPIE software for listing social relationship strengths.

Step III: Identify Recommended Interventions

Practitioners who wish to generate an intervention plan may record recommended interventions, the intervention goals, the priority of the intervention, the practitioner or agency that might provide the recommended interventions, and the expected outcome. This step is often done after all problems have been identified and the practitioner has been able to study the findings on all the PIE Factors.

Recording Factor II: Environmental Situations (Social Support System Problems)

Environmental situations are divided into six categories encompassing most of a community's array of social institutions and social support systems (see chapter 4):

- Basic Needs
- Health and Safety
- Education and Training
- Voluntary Groups
- Judicial and Legal
- Affectional Support Groups

In each of these categories there are **types** of problems. For example, the Basic Needs category includes problems such as lack of or inadequate food, shelter, transportation, employment, and income. The Judicial and Legal category includes lack of or inadequate police service, courts, detention facilities, legal services, and so forth. It is important to note that Factor II is not an assessment of the total community in which the client lives. Rather, it is an identification of those social institutions and networks with which the client is currently having difficulty and that are seen as contributing to the client's problems in social functioning.

Discrimination in social institutions is an important component of Factor II. Refer to chapter 4 for descriptions and definitions and how to record discrimination.

Follow the steps below to record Factor II findings:

Step I: Identify the Category of the Environmental Problem and the of Problem in Each Category

1. Identify all the **Environmental Situations (Social Support System Problems)** that the practitioner and the client observe at the time of the assessment. For example: Shelter.
2. Identify the type of problem in each category where a problem is identified. For example: Absence of adequate shelter in the community.
3. Classify the **severity** of each situation using the Severity Index
4. Record the **length of time** that the client reports experiencing a problem in each category using the Duration Index.
5. If **discrimination** is identified in any category, record this finding indicating the social institution in which it is observed and the type of discrimination using the Discrimination type discussed in chapter 4.

Step II: Identify Community Resources

1. Identify all the social institutions or support systems in the client's community that are a potential resource for helping with the client's situation. For example, for a client who is homeless, the presence of an effective housing program would be a Basic Needs, Shelter strength. For a client needing treatment for a mental illness the presence of an effective mental health service would be noted as Health, Safety, and Social Service strength. Often there will be more than one strength.

    Note: Since Factor II identifies the problem as existing within the environment and not within the client, the Coping Index is not used in Factor II. If, however, the client is involved in addressing the environmental situation this fact can be noted under "Recommended Interventions." This step is often done after all problems have been identified.

Step III: Identify Interventions

Practitioners who are generating an intervention plan may record the goal, the recommended intervention, the practitioner or agency that might provide the recommended interventions, and the expected outcome. As noted on Factor I, this step is often made after all PIE Factor problems have been identified.

Recording Factor III: Mental Health Conditions

Step I: Identify the Mental Health Condition

1. List the DSM[1] Axis I and II diagnoses or clinical syndromes using other systems (as diagnosed by a licensed practitioner).
2. Enter **severity** of the disorder using the Severity Index.
3. Enter **duration** using the Duration Index

Step II: Identify Client Strengths

1. Enter your estimate of the client's **coping ability** using the Coping Index.
2. Enter the presence or absence of other client strengths.

Step III: Identify Interventions

1. As in Factors I and II enter recommended intervention, practitioner or agency, goal, and expected outcome.

Recording Factor IV: Physical Health Conditions

Step I: Identify the Client's Physical Health Conditions

1. List the client's Physical Health Conditions[2] indicating whether the diagnosis is by a licensed practitioner or by client report

---

[1] The ICD-10 (International Classification of Diseases) may be used by those not using the DSM (Diagnostic and Statistical Manual).
[2] Refer to the DSM Axis III, the ICD (International Classification of Diseases), or the ICF (International Classification of Functioning, Disability, and Health).

2. List other health conditions reported by the client or others.
3. Enter **severity** of each condition using Severity Index.
4. Enter **duration** of each condition using Duration Index.

Step II: Identify Strengths

1. Enter your estimate of the client's **coping ability** for each condition.
2. Enter other client strengths.

Step III: Identify Interventions

1. Enter recommended intervention for each condition and its priority
2. Enter recommended practitioner or agency, goal, and expected outcome.

Recording Case History, Dynamics, and Comments

The PIE System is designed to produce a holistic picture of the client's situation that is both comprehensive and succinct. This may leave the practitioner wanting to explain or add to the findings. To do this both the CompuPIE software and the PIE Worksheet contain space for augmenting the succinct PIE problem descriptions. Thus the practitioner may:

- record a summary of the case in narrative form.
- record case dynamics and provide an opinion on the interactions among the PIE factors. (Practitioner may use a theoretical framework to explain the client's condition).
- note that other problems may exist in certain Factors, but there is insufficient information to identify them at the time of the assessment.
- provide an opinion about the priorities for intervention.

Compiling the Assessment Summary

Using the PIE Worksheet

The PIE Worksheet contains all the elements of the PIE system and serves as a paper print form for recording and summarizing case findings. After all the entries are made on the PIE Worksheet, the practitioner manually transfers these data to the Assessment Summary sheet.

Using the CompuPIE Software

The CompuPIE software program has the same content as the PIE Worksheet. Assessment findings are recorded electronically by scrolling the menus and clicking on each problem, condition, or situation along with their qualifiers. The software program will summarize the findings and recommendations for intervention.

Digital Coding

On both the PIE Worksheet and the CompuPIE software client problems and conditions can be recorded digitally. There are code numbers for all problems and conditions listed in the PIE System. Thus, findings can be recorded in numerical codes as well as in narrative form. The coding system is explained in appendix 3. Using the numerical codes on the Worksheet can slow the recording process and is not encouraged unless case findings are being used in research. The CompuPIE software automatically changes the problem listings into numerical codes and reports the findings in both narrative and numerical code format.

Planning Interventions, Setting Priorities, Taking Action

The time pressures in clinical practice often make it difficult to conduct the careful comprehensive assessment that the PIE System outlines. Yet, the importance of a careful, comprehensive assessment cannot be over emphasized.

The PIE Assessment Summary provides a comprehensive picture of problems presented by the client in succinct format. In planning interventions and setting priorities, review and study your findings as an important first step (ideally in collaboration with your client). Study the array of problems before making recommendations. Problems in Social Role functioning can be related to problems in the environment, mental and physical health conditions, and the client's strengths and resources.

Set priorities by studying the severity and coping ability indicators. These may influence your decision on where and when to start interventions and with whom. A problem noted as "severe" and with "poor coping ability" has a high priority for early intervention. Conversely, a "chronic problem" with "moderate coping ability" is of lower priority. "Outstanding coping ability" indicates that no intervention may be necessary.

By using the PIE System, you and your client will have gained a clearer understanding of the problems, the possible interventions, and the order in which the problems might be effectively addressed. Now you and the client are ready to implement the plan. Whereas the helping process occurs simultaneously with developing rapport and a good relationship, your ability to work effectively with your client will be greatly enhanced by doing the careful and comprehensive PIE assessment.

Updating and Amending the PIE Assessment

The PIE System assessment is intended to be a tool in helping the client. As such, assessment findings may be modified or amended as the practitioner gains further information about client problems and strengths. Perhaps new problems emerge as old ones diminish in severity.

Or new strengths are identified. Perhaps the recommended interventions are inadequate and need to be changed. For whatever reason, the PIE assessment can be changed to reflect any new information gained in the course of working with the client. The PIE Worksheet Summary can be edited or updated. The CompuPIE software can be amended to accommodate new information. Both have mechanisms for recording an interim assessment or a final assessment.

Remember that the goal in the PIE system is to help the client to achieve optimum social functioning. By doing a careful assessment using the PIE system you (and the client) will have a clear comprehensive picture of what is needed to reach this goal and how you and the client can help bring it about.

REFERENCES

American Psychiatric Association. (2000). *Diagnostic and statistical manual of mental disorders* (4th ed.). Washington, DC: American Psychiatric Press.

World Health Organization, (2007). *International classification of diseases-10 revision-clinical modification* Available at: http://www.who.int/classifications/apps/icd/icd10online/

World Health Organization. (2001). *International classification of functioning, disability and health.* Available from: www.disabilitaincifre.it/documenti/ICF_18.pdf .

PIE SYSTEM WORKSHEET

Client Name: _____
Client Alias: _____
Client Address: _____
Phone Number: _____
Practitioner: _____
Referred by: _____
Assessment Date: _____
Assessed by: _____

Client I. D. #: _____
Date of Birth: _____
Gender: _____
Marital Status: _____
Ethnicity: _____
Occupation: _____
Other Info: _____

FACTOR I: SOCIAL ROLE and RELATIONSHIP FUNCTIONING

PROBLEM IDENTIFICATION				STRENGTHS		INTERVENTION PLAN			
Role	Type	Severity	Duration	Coping Ability	Other Strengths	Goal	Intervention	Refer To	Expected Outcome
□ Family									
□ Parent									
□ Spouse									
□ Child (Adult)									
□ Sibling									
□ Extended Family									
□ Interpersonal									
□ Lover									
□ Friend									
□ Neighbor									
□ Member									
□ Other:									

PROBLEM IDENTIFICATION				STRENGTHS		INTERVENTION PLAN			
Role	Type	Severity	Duration	Coping Ability	Other Strengths	Goal	Intervention	Refer To	Expected Outcome
☐ Occupational									
☐ Paid Worker									
☐ Homemaker									
☐ Volunteer									
☐ Student									
☐ Other:									
☐ Special Life Situation									
☐ Consumer									
☐ Caretaker									
☐ Inpatient Client									
☐ Outpatient Client									
☐ Probationer/ Parolee									
☐ Prisoner									
☐ Legal Immigrant									
☐ Undocumented Immigrant									
☐ Refugee Immigrant									
☐ Other:									

USE ABBREVIATIONS OR NUMBERS ON ASSESSMENT FORM

RELATIONSHIP TYPE INDEX

1	Power	PWR	6	Isolation	ISO
2	Ambivalence	AMB	7	Oppressed	OPR
3	Responsibility	RES	10	Mixed	MXD
4	Dependency	DEP	11	Undetermined	UND
5	Loss	LOS	12	Other (specify) ___	

DURATION INDEX

1	5 or more years	Y: 5+
2	1–5 years	Y: 1–5
3	6–12 months	M: 6–12
4	1–6 months	M: 1–6
5	1–4 weeks	W: 1–4

SEVERITY INDEX

1	Low	L
2	Moderate	M
3	High	H
4	Very high	H+
5	Catastrophic	C

COPING INDEX

1	Outstanding	A
2	Above average	B
3	Adequate	C
4	Somewhat inadequate	D
5	Inadequate	F
6	Unable to judge at this time	I

STRENGTH INDEX

1	Notable Strengths	N
2	Possible strengths	P

FACTOR II: ENVIRONMENTAL SITUATIONS (SOCIAL SUPPORT SYSTEMS)

1. Basic Needs
2. Education and Training
3. Judicial and Legal
4. Health, Safety and Social Services
5. Voluntary Association
6. Affectional Support

1. BASIC NEEDS SYSTEM PROBLEM (Food, Shelter, Employment, Income, Transportation, Discrimination)

PROBLEM IDENTIFICATION				RESOURCES	IDENTIFICATION PLAN			
Type	Severity	Duration	Discrimination	Resource	Goal	Intervention	Refer To	Expected Outcome
☐ Food/Nutrition								
☐ Lack of regular food supply in community								
☐ Lack of food/water supply								
☐ Nutritionally inadequate food supply								
☐ Other:								
☐ Shelter								
☐ Absence of shelter								
☐ Substandard or inadequate shelter								
☐ Other:								
☐ Employment								
☐ No work available in community								
☐ Insufficient Employment								
☐ Inappropriate Employment								
☐ Other:								

PROBLEM IDENTIFICATION				RESOURCES	IDENTIFICATION PLAN			
Type	Severity	Duration	Discrimination	Resource	Goal	Intervention	Refer To	Expected Outcome
☐ Economic Resources								
☐ Insufficient resources for basic sustenance								
☐ Insufficient resources to provide needed services								
☐ Regulatory barriers								
☐ Other:								
☐ Transportation								
☐ No transportation to job/needed services								
☐ Inadequate transportation								
☐ Other:								

2. EDUCATION AND TRAINING SYSTEM PROBLEM (Schools, Training Facilities)

PROBLEM IDENTIFICATION				RESOURCES	IDENTIFICATION PLAN			
Type	Severity	Duration	Discrimination	Resource	Goal	Intervention	Refer To	Expected Outcome
☐ Education and Training								
☐ Lack of education/ training facilities								
☐ Lack of adequate or appropriate facilities								
☐ Lack of culturally relevant facilities								
☐ Regulatory barriers								
☐ Absence of support services								
☐ Other:								

3. JUDICIAL AND LEGAL SYSTEM PROBLEM (Police, Courts, Prosecution/Defense, Probation/Parole, Detention Facilities)

PROBLEM IDENTIFICATION				RESOURCES	IDENTIFICATION PLAN			
Type	Severity	Duration	Discrimination	Resource	Goal	Intervention	Refer To	Expected Outcome
☐ Justice and Legal System								
☐ Lack of police services								
☐ Lack of relevant police services								
☐ Lack of confidence in police services								
☐ Lack of adequate prosecution/defense								
☐ Lack of adequate probation/parole								
☐ Other:								

4. HEALTH, SAFETY, AND SOCIAL SERVICES SYSTEM PROBLEM

PROBLEM IDENTIFICATION				RESOURCES	IDENTIFICATION PLAN			
Type	Severity	Duration	Discrimination	Resource	Goal	Intervention	Refer To	Expected Outcome
☐ Health/Mental Health								
☐ Absence of adequate health services								
☐ Regulatory barriers to health services								
☐ Inaccessibility of health services								
☐ Absence of support services/Health Services								
☐ Absence of adequate mental health services								
☐ Regulatory barriers to mental health services								

PROBLEM IDENTIFICATION				RESOURCES	IDENTIFICATION PLAN			
Type	Severity	Duration	Discrimination	Resource	Goal	Intervention	Refer To	Expected Outcome
☐ Inaccessibility of mental health services								
☐ Absence of support services/Mental health								
☐ Other:								
☐ Safety								
☐ Violence or crime in neighborhood								
☐ Unsafe working conditions								
☐ Unsafe conditions in home								
☐ Absence of adequate safety services								
☐ Natural disaster								
☐ Human-created disaster								
☐ Other:								
☐ Social Services								
☐ Absence of adequate social services								
☐ Regulatory barriers to social services								
☐ Inaccessibility of social services								
☐ Absence of support services/Social services								
☐ Other (specify):								

5. VOLUNTARY ASSOCIATION SYSTEM PROBLEM (Religious Organizations, Social Support Groups, Community Groups)

PROBLEM IDENTIFICATION				RESOURCES	IDENTIFICATION PLAN				
Type	Severity	Duration	Discrimination	Resource	Goal	Intervention	Refer To	Expected Outcome	
☐ Religious Groups									
☐ Lack of religious group of choice									
☐ Lack of acceptance of religious values or beliefs									
☐ Other:									
☐ Community Groups									
☐ Lack of community support group of choice									
☐ Lack acceptance of community group of choice									
☐ Other:									

6. AFFECTIONAL SUPPORT SYSTEM PROBLEM (Family, Friends, Natural Helping Networks)

PROBLEM IDENTIFICATION				RESOURCES	IDENTIFICATION PLAN			
Type	Severity	Duration	Discrimination	Resource	Goal	Intervention	Refer To	Expected Outcome
☐ Affectional Support System								
☐ Absence of affectional support system								
☐ Support system inadequate to meet affectional needs								
☐ Excessively involved support system								
☐ Other:								

USE ABBREVIATIONS OR NUMBERS ON ASSESSMENT FORM

DISCRIMINATION INDEX

01	Age	AGE	08	Veteran status	VET
02	Ethnicity, color, or language	ETH	09	Dependency status	DEP
03	Religion	RLG	10	Disability status	DIS
04	Gender	GEN	11	Marital status	MAR
05	Sexual orientation	SXR	12	Body size	BOD
06	Lifestyle	LIFE	13	Political affiliation	POL
07	Non Citizen	NCT	14	Other:_____	

DURATION INDEX

1	5 or more years	Y: 5+
2	1–5 years	Y: 1–5
3	6–12 months	M: 6–12
4	1–6 months	M: 1–6
5	1–4 weeks	W: 1–4

SEVERITY INDEX

1	Low	L
2	Moderate	M
3	High	H
4	Very high	H+
5	Catastrophic	C

STRENGTH INDEX

1	Notable Strengths	N
2	Possible strengths	P

FACTOR III: MENTAL HEALTH CONDITIONS

PROBLEM IDENTIFICATION					STRENGTHS		INTERVENTION PLAN			
Diagnosis	Professional Diagnosis	Client Report	Severity	Duration	Coping Ability	Other Strengths	Goal	Intervention	Refer To	Expected Outcome
DSM Axis I										
1.										
2.										
DSM Axis II										
1.										
2.										
Other Diagnostic System Diagnosis:										
1.										
2.										

USE ABBREVIATIONS OR NUMBERS ON ASSESSMENT FORM

DURATION INDEX

1	5 or more years	Y: 5+
2	1–5 years	Y: 1–5
3	6–12 months	M: 6–12
4	1–6 months	M: 1–6
5	1–4 weeks	W: 1–4

SEVERITY INDEX

1	Low	L
2	Moderate	M
3	High	H
4	Very high	H+
5	Catastrophic	C

COPING INDEX

1	Outstanding	A
2	Above average	B
3	Adequate	C
4	Somewhat inadequate	D
5	Inadequate	F
6	Unable to judge at this time	I

STRENGTH INDEX

1	Notable Strengths	N
2	Possible strengths	P

FACTOR IV: PHYSICAL HEALTH CONDITIONS

	PROBLEM IDENTIFICATION				STRENGTHS		INTERVENTION PLAN			
Diagnosis	Professional Diagnosis	Client Report	Severity	Duration	Coping Ability	Other Strengths	Goal	Intervention	Refer To	Expected Outcome
Physical Health Conditions										
1.										
2.										
3.										
4.										
Other Conditions										
1.										
2.										

USE ABBREVIATIONS OR NUMBERS ON ASSESSMENT FORM

DURATION INDEX

1	5 or more years	Y: 5+
2	1–5 years	Y: 1–5
3	6–12 months	M: 6–12
4	1–6 months	M: 1–6
5	1–4 weeks	W: 1–4

SEVERITY INDEX

1	Low	L
2	Moderate	M
3	High	H
4	Very high	H+
5	Catastrophic	C

COPING INDEX

1	Outstanding	A
2	Above average	B
3	Adequate	C
4	Somewhat inadequate	D
5	Inadequate	F
6	Unable to judge at this time	I

STRENGTH INDEX

1	Notable Strengths	N
2	Possible strengths	P

ASSESSMENT SUMMARY & INTERVENTION PLAN

Client Name: _____

Client Alias: _____

Client Address: _____

Phone Number: _____

Practitioner: _____

Referred by: _____

Client I. D. #: _____

Date of Birth: _____

Gender: _____

Marital Status: _____

Ethnicity: _____

Occupation: _____

ASSESSMENT FINDINGS	RECOMMENDED INTERVENTION	PRIORITY
Factor I: Social Role and Relationship Functioning Problems		
1		
2.		
3.		
Factor I: Social Role and Relationship Functioning Strengths		
Factor II: Environmental Situations (Social Support Systems)		
1.		
2.		
3.		
Factor II: Environmental Situations (Social Support Systems) Strengths		

Factor III: Mental Health Functioning	
DSM Axis I:	
DSM Axis II:	
Other Diagnostic System Diagnosis:	
Factor III: Mental Health Functioning Strengths	
Factor IV: Physical Health Conditions	
1.	
2.	
3.	
Factor IV: Physical Health Strengths	

CLINICAL NOTES / CLIENT DATA / CASE ANALYSIS / INTERPRETATION OF FINDINGS

Clinical Notes / Client Data / Case Analysis / Interpretation of Findings

CHAPTER 9

Case Examples Using PIE

The following case vignettes from various settings have been analyzed using PIE and illustrate the process of thinking through how to assess a client on each of the four Factors. The first two case vignettes (Martha Brown and Sam Palm) are presented again in appendix 8 to demonstrate the use of the PIE worksheets and to provide an example of a completed assessment generated by CompuPIE.

Family Services Agency

Mrs. Brown, a 33-year-old divorced mother of three children, was referred to a family services agency by a counselor at her son's school. Her eldest son, age 10, has been getting into fights more frequently at school, especially during the past several months. Mrs. Brown reported that her son has been difficult to manage since her divorce two years ago. She reported that he has frequent temper outbursts and bullies younger children and that these behaviors have also been increasing at home during the past several months. Ms. Brown reported a history of domestic violence in the marriage. She recently learned that her ex-husband is planning to remarry and believes that this may be one of the reasons for the increase in her son's behavior problems. Mrs. Brown also expressed concerned about her daughter, age 12, whom she describes as shy and doing poorly academically in school. Mrs. Brown reported that she is feeling overwhelmed and stated: "It is a struggle for me just to get up in the morning."

During the past three months Mrs. Brown has been dating a man whom she describes as kind, but added she does not know if she wants to continue this relationship because her son does not like him and this has contributed to arguments between her and her son.

Mrs. Brown's situation is aggravated by financial problems. Since her divorce she has had to move to a smaller apartment in a less desirable and less safe neighborhood. Her ex-husband pays only $200 a month in child support and he is sporadic in his payments. Also, one month ago due to cutbacks at her place of employment, her work hours were reduced to only 25 hours per week. She has been unable to find additional work and is worried about being able to make ends meet financially.

PIE Assessment

There are a number of areas of difficulty Mrs. Brown is presently experiencing. The primary problem revolves around dealing with her children's behavioral problems. Thus, Factor I would be described as a Parent Role Problem, Responsibility type. After your initial assessment, you determine that the disruption this causes is moderate (the severity index = 2), the duration of the problem is one to five years (duration = 2), and her coping capacity is somewhat inadequate (coping index = 4), because she has made little headway in resolving this problem.

Another problem she is experiencing is her ambivalent relationship with her boyfriend (Lover Role Problem, Ambivalence type). For her Lover Role problem, you determine that the disruption it causes is low (severity index = 1), the duration rating is one to six months (duration = 4) because the problem has been going on for three months, and her coping capacity is judged by you as somewhat inadequate (coping index = 4).

Another problem Mrs. Brown is experiencing is coping with the divorce. Although it occurred two years ago, Mrs. Brown. is still experiencing problems related to it, including dealing with her children's reaction to the divorce as well as the change in lifestyle. Thus, this client's Factor I statement would appear as follows:

Factor I   Parent Role Problem, Responsibility
            type, moderate severity, 1 to 5 years
            duration, somewhat inadequate coping
            capacity (primary problem).

            Lover Role Problem, Ambivalence type,
            low severity, 1 to 6 months' duration,
            somewhat inadequate coping capacity.

            Spousal Role Problem, Mixed type,
            loss and victimization, moderate severi-
            ty, 1 to 5 years, somewhat inadequate
            coping capacity.

With regard to strengths, although Mrs. Brown is
experiencing problems in her role as a parent, this is also a
notable strength. Mrs. Brown's decision to leave her husband was largely based on her concerns that her children
were being negatively affected by the violence.

You determine that the client's difficulties are
aggravated by the lack of job opportunities in her community and she is not eligible for public assistance. You identify this as a Basic Needs System Problem, lack of economic resources to provide for herself and her dependents.
You judge this as causing a moderate degree of disruption
(severity index = 3). Since this economic problem has been
going on for four weeks, the duration rating is 4. Thus, this
client's Factor II statement would appear as follows:

Factor II   Basic Needs System Problem, insuffi-
             cient economic resources in the com-
             munity to provide for client and
             dependents, moderate severity, 1 to 4
             weeks' duration.

You determine that this client is depressed and
meets the criteria for a single episode of Major Depression
as described in the *Diagnostic and Statistical Manual
of Mental Disorders, Fourth Edition* (DSM-IV TR)
(American Psychiatric Association, 2000). The severity is
moderate and she has been experiencing these symptoms
for the past 6six to eightweeks. However, given the
client's history of spousal abuse, you want to explore further the possibility that the client's symptoms are a conse-
quence of having experienced spousal abuse. You determine that she does not have a personality disorder or
developmental problem. Therefore, this client's Factor 1II
statement would appear as follows:

Factor III

Axis I   296.22   Major Depression, single
                    episode, moderate

          309.81   Rule Out Posttraumatic
                    Stress Disorder

Axis II   V71.09   No diagnosis on Axis II.

Finally, the client reports frequent headaches which
affect her functioning. It is possible that these headaches
may be the result of head injuries sustained during a bat-
tering incident. Mrs. Brown states the headaches worsen
when she is under stress and that during the past month
they have become more severe. Therefore, Factor IV
would be recorded as follows:

Factor IV   Headaches (by client report), high
             severity.

The complete multifactorial description of this
client on PIE follows:

Factor I   Parent Role Problem, Responsibility
            type, moderate severity, 1 to 5 years'
            duration, somewhat inadequate coping
            capacity (primary problem)

            Lover Role Problem, Ambivalence type,
            low severity, 1 to 6 months' duration,
            somewhat inadequate coping capacity.

            Spousal Role Problem, Mixed type
            (loss and victimization)

            Notable Strengths: Parent Role

Factor II   Basic Needs System Problem, insuffi-
            cient economic resources in the commu-
            nity to provide for self and dependents,
            high severity, 1 to 4 weeks' duration.

Factor III

Axis I   296.22   Major Depression, single
                    episode, moderate

          309.81   R/O PTSD disorder

Axis II   V71.09   No diagnosis on Axis II

Factor IV   Headaches, high (by client report)

Criminal Justice

Sam Palm is a 40-year-old African American parolee who
was referred to a community agency whose goal is to
reduce recidivism by facilitating parolees' re entry
process. After serving seven years in prison for a series of

drug offenses and aggravated assault, he was released two weeks ago and is dealing with life "outside." Sam resides at the local YMCA residential program, attends AA and has found a temporary part-time job at a local restaurant. While in prison he obtained his GED and received training in auto mechanics and he would like to find a mechanics job. Sam reports, however, that when prospective employers find out about his record they don't hire him. He reports feeling "a lot of anxiety" but believes he is turning his life around. He reports being drug free and wants to submit to random drug testing to prove himself. Sam has few social supports. He has no contact with his parents whom he described as physically abusive toward him as a child, and states that his old friends are all gang members, drug users and "not worth knowing." His major support is his girlfriend who visited him frequently while he was in prison. Another support he identifies is his Bible. Sam reports that after he gets a job and becomes more stable, he wants to begin a new life with his girlfriend.

PIE Assessment

Your assessment is that Sam is experiencing anxiety due to the role change from prisoner to parolee (severity index = 3). He was released from prison two weeks ago, so the duration rating is 1 to 4 weeks (duration = 5), and from what you know of his history you judge his coping skills to be adequate (coping index = 3). This client's Factor I statement would be written as follows:

> Factor I   Probationer/Parolee Role Problem, Loss type, severity is high, 1 to 4 weeks duration, adequate coping skills.
>
> Notable strength is his relationship with girlfriend (Lover Role)

Although the community has many problems related to the economic system, such as inadequate housing, and transportation, you conclude that the main economic system problem is the discrimination against parolees in obtaining adequate employment. This problem is of high severity in this community (severity index = 3) and although it has been going on for many years, Sly has been experiencing this problem for 1 to 4 weeks (5). Thus, this client's Factor II statement would read as follows:

> Factor II   Basic Needs System Problem, Discrimination, other discrimination (parole status), high severity, 1 to 4 weeks' duration.

You determine that although Sam is experiencing anxiety he does not meet the criteria for an Anxiety Disorder nor does he suffer from any other mental, personality, or developmental disorder. Thus, his Factor III statement would appear as follows:

> Factor III
>
> Axis I   V71.09   No diagnosis on Axis I.
>
> Axis II   V71.09   No diagnosis on Axis II.

A particular strength that has helped Sam stay sober and a key factor motivating him to turn his life around is his spiritual beliefs. Thus, a Notable Strength would be his spirituality. Finally the client's medical record reports that he has severe asthma, which worsens when he is under stress. Thus, his Factor IV statement would be the following:

> Factor IV   Severe asthma (by Dr. X).

A complete multifactorial description of this client would be written as follows:

> Factor I   Probationer /Parolee Role Problem, Loss type, high severity, less than two weeks' duration, adequate coping skills.
>
> Notable strengths (Lover Role: relationship with girlfriend)
>
> Factor II   Basic Needs System Problem, Discrimination, other discrimination (parole status), high severity, 1 to 4 weeks' duration.
>
> Factor III
>
> Axis I   V71.09   No diagnosis on Axis I.
>
> Substance Dependence in full remission
>
> Axis II   V71.09   No diagnosis on Axis II.
>
> Notable strengths: Spirituality
>
> Factor IV   Severe asthma (by Dr. X).

Medical Social Work

Luisa is a 20-year-old single Mexican American woman who is returning to the medical clinic eight weeks after she was raped. She reports that she is not feeling well, has missed her period, and thinks she may be pregnant.

Right after she was raped, Luisa was brought to the clinic by her sister and was given counseling on emergency contraception. She started to use the morning-after regiment two days after the initial interview. However after taking the first set of pills she developed severe nausea, vomited several times during the night, and the next morning thought she was too sick to take the second set of pills. On this second visit, the nurse performed a urine pregnancy test and it came back positive. Louisa describes herself as a devout Catholic and stated she does not know what she should do because she has always been against abortion.

Luisa lives with her older sister, her sister's husband, and their two children. Luisa works as a secretary for a law firm. She was on vacation when the rape occurred and returned to work two weeks after the rape but did not want anyone to know what had happened. Since her return to work she has been performing poorly and is worried she might be fired. She reported having difficulty sleeping and concentrating. She also reports she has been very moody, at times feeling very depressed and other times lashing out at people for no apparent reason.

PIE Assessment

Your assessment is that Luisa is experiencing a very high degree of disruption in her life (severity index = 4) in several roles including Lover Role, Paid Worker Role-Paid Economic and Member Role (Catholic Church). The rape occurred eight weeks, so the duration rating is 4. You determine that her coping skills for Lover Role, Worker Role, and Member Role Problems are inadequate, thus her coping rating is 4 for each. This client's Factor I statement would be written as follows:

> Factor I   Lover Role, Victimization type, high severity 1 to 6 months duration inadequate coping (primary problem)
>
> Paid Worker Role-Economic Problem, Responsibility type, high severity, 1 to 4 weeks' duration, inadequate coping skills
>
> Member Role, Ambivalent type, high severity, 1 to 4 weeks' duration, somewhat inadequate coping skills

With regard to Social Role Functioning strengths, this client's relationship with her sister is a notable strength. Luisa has a close and supportive relationship with her sister who has been especially helpful to her in the past two months.

There are no problems on Factor II. In fact, because there are a number of free community services providing both short-and long-term treatment to victims of sexual assault, this is a community asset or resource.

> Factor II   No problems
>
> Strengths/   Community program for
> Assets   victims of sexual assault

This client is experiencing severe anxiety and has numerous symptoms indicative of diagnosis of Post-traumatic Stress Disorder, including nightmares, sleep problems, depression, flashbacks to the rape, bouts of anger, difficulty concentrating, , and irritable mood. She does not have a personality or a developmental disorder. Therefore, her Factor III statement would be written as follows:

> Factor III
>
> Axis I   309.81   Posttraumatic Stress Disorder
>
> Axis II   No diagnosis on Axis II.

Luisa has a number of strengths on Factor III. She has insight into her difficulties and has a history of resilience.

With regard to Factor IV, this woman's Factor IV listing would be:

> Factor IV Pregnancy as a result of rape

A complete multifactorial PIE report on this client would appear as follows:

> Factor I
>
> Lover Role, Victimization type, high severity, 1 to 6 months duration, inadequate coping (primary problem)
>
> Paid Worker Role-Economic Problem, Responsibility type, high severity, 1 to 4 weeks' duration, inadequate coping skills.
>
> Member Role (Catholic Church member), Ambivalence type, high severity, 4 weeks' duration, adequate coping skills.
>
> Notable Strength: Sibling Role

Factor II	No problems	
	Strengths/ Assets	Community programs for victims of sexual assault

Factor III

Axis I	309.81	Posttraumatic Stress Disorder
Axis II	V71.09	No diagnosis on Axis II

Notable strengths: intelligence, resilience

Factor IV

Pregnancy as a result of rape

Psychiatric Inpatient

Cory, a 26-year-old single male with a prominent tattoo on his forehead, was admitted to the state hospital three days ago with an acute episode of schizophrenia. Corey had stopped taking his medication, was not sleeping, and had become increasingly disorientated during the preceding several weeks. Cory was also carrying a knife in his backpack, stating that because he was a member of the KKK, members of a nonwhite organization were trying to kill him. He reported that if he were found, he would be tortured and so it was best to kill himself.

Corey had his first psychotic episode when he was 20. At that time he was attending a local community college and began hearing voices telling him he was "God's ambassador on a special mission to change the social order and stop criminal activity." Since age 20, Cory has had four hospitalizations and has been unable to work or maintain any stable social relationships.

Cory had been living with his grandmother until approximately three months ago when he moved in with friends whom his grandmother described as skinheads. The grandmother reported that Corey would come by her home almost daily to eat.

Since his hospitalization three days ago, Corey has refused all medication and becomes either self-injurious or violent to staff when they attempt to administer it. Corey's grandmother reports she has become frightened of Corey's behavior and thinks it would be best if he went to a group home or residential facility upon his discharge from the hospital

PIE Assessment

Your assessment is that Cory's primary problem is that he is suffering from paranoid schizophrenia (Factor III). Because he does not take his prescribed medication and engages in violent behaviors toward self and others that causes him to be re hospitalized, you determine that this young man's primary Factor I problem—Inpatient/Client Role Problem, Dependency type is of very high severity. This client's Factor I statement would be written as follows:

Factor I	Inpatient/Client Role Problem, Dependency type, severity is high, 1 to 4 weeks' duration, inadequate coping skills.

Corey's problems are largely affected by the lack adequate mental health services available in his community. There are few group homes or residential services in his community that serve clients with a persistent mental illness. This problem has been going on for many years, therefore his Factor II statement would appear as follows:

Factor II	Health, Safety, and Social Services System Problem, absence of adequate mental health services, high severity, more than five years' duration.

As stated, Cory's primary problem is his mental illness. Factor III would be written as follows

Factor III

Axis I	295.32	Schizophrenia, paranoid type, high severity
Axis II	V71.09	No diagnosis on Axis II.

Corey has a number of areas of strength, including intelligence as well as creativity. Specifically, Cory is a good chess player and excellent at video games. He is also a good artist and when on medication he has been able to produce detailed and well-executed portraits.

A physical examination reveals that this client has scabies. Therefore, this client's Factor IV statement would appear as follows:

Factor IV Scabies (by Dr. Z)

A complete multifactorial report on this client would appear as follows:

Factor I	Inpatient/Client Role Problem, Dependency type, very high severity, more than five years' duration, no coping skills.
	Notable strengths: Relationship with grandmother

Factor II Health, Safety, and Social Services System Problem, absence of adequate mental health services, high severity, more than five years' duration.

Factor III

Axis I   295.32   Schizophrenia, paranoid type, chronic.

Axis II   V71.09   No diagnosis on Axis II.

          Notable strengths: intelligence and creativity

Factor IV Scabies (by Dr. Z)

Rehabilitation

Ann, a 27-year-old white female, was in a motorcycle accident with her 29-year-old live-in boyfriend three weeks ago. They both had been drinking and were riding with a group when a car tried to taunt them by swerving toward their bike. Her boyfriend lost control of his bike and ran into a tree. He died immediately. Ann experienced a severe concussion and her leg required amputation. Two days ago, she was discharged from the hospital to the rehab center. Since being hospitalized, none of her biker friends have visited her. Her present supports are her father and stepmother who have been visiting her regularly.

Ann is demonstrating signs of complicated grief. She reports she wishes she had died and is unmotivated to participate in the rehabilitation program.

It is anticipated that Ann will be in rehab for approximately seven to -10 days. Because she has no health insurance this is the maximum stay Medicaid will pay for. Ann will then be discharged to her father and stepmother's home. Ann reports she and her father have never really gotten along and does not really want to live with them but sees no alternative.

PIE Assessment

Your assessment is that Ann has experienced a very high to catastrophic degree of disruption in her life affecting numerous social roles, the foremost including Spousal Role, Inpatient Role, and Child Role, as well as Paid Worker Role, although the latter role problem is not directly affecting Ann at this time. The accident occurred three weeks ago, so the duration rating is 5. You determine that her coping skills for each of these roles are range from inadequate to somewhat inadequate. This client's Factor I statement would be written as follows:

Factor I   Spouse Role Problem, Loss type, very high severity, 1 to 4 weeks' duration, inadequate coping skills.

           Inpatient/Client Role, Isolation type, very high severity, 1 to 4 weeks' duration, inadequate coping skills

           Child Role, Dependency type, high severity, 1 to 4 weeks' duration, somewhat inadequate coping skills

You determine that there are several environmental conditions affecting Ann's situation. She has no health insurance and will be allowed to stay at rehab only until has her new prosthetic. She will be discharged to her father and stepmother's care where there are no rehab services. There are also no available mental heath services to help her cope with the many losses in her life.

Factor II Health, Safety, and Social Services System, Lack of health insurance, lack of rehabilitation services, lack of low cost mental heath services, high severity, 1 to 4 weeks duration

You determine that Ann is experiencing severe depression. Presently she is not exhibiting symptoms of any other mental disorder, so her Factor III statement would be described as follows:

Factor III

Axis I   296.23   Major Depression, single episode, severe (principal diagnosis)

          305.00   Alcohol abuse

Axis II   No diagnosis on Axis II

From her medical records, this client's Factor IV statement would be written as follows:

Factor IV Post-concussive syndrome (as reported by Dr. Y)

           Amputee—loss of right leg from motorcycle accident

A complete multifactorial PIE report on this client would then be written as follows:

Factor I   Spouse Role Problem, Loss type, high
            severity, inadequate coping skills, 1 to
            4 weeks duration.

            Inpatient/Client Role, Isolation type,
            very high severity, 1 to 4 weeks' dura-
            tion, inadequate coping skills

            Child Role, Dependency type, high
            severity, 1 to 4 weeks' duration, some-
            what inadequate coping skills

Factor II   Health, Safety, and Social Services
            System, Lack of health insurance, lack
            of rehabilitation services, high severity,
            1 to 4 weeks' duration.

Factor III

Axis I   296.23   Major Depression, single
                        episode, severe (principal
                        diagnosis). R/O PTSD

            305.00   Alcohol abuse

Axis II   V71.09   No diagnosis on Axis II.

Factor IV   Post-concussive syndrome
            (as reported by Dr. Y)

            Amputee—loss of right leg from
            motorcycle accident

Outpatient Psychiatric Clinic

Sheng is a 33-year-old married Hmong woman, with
three children ages four, seven, and nine years old. She
was referred to the outpatient department by a friend. She
describes herself as very close with her family, but stated
she cannot confide in them about her situation. For the
past four years, Sheng worked in a clerical position for a
medium size company. Approximately six months ago,
her boss began to make sexual overtures to her including
touching her inappropriately. She attempted to confront
the issue by speaking both to her boss and her boss's
supervisor. However, shortly after the incident, she was
fired. Sheng has been unemployed for the past five
months.

Since then, her overall level of functioning has significantly decreased. She reports difficulty sleeping and
has had reoccurring memories and flashbacks relating to
the incident. Sheng also reports mood swings, and stated
that she is easily irritated and gets angry very quickly.

The incident has caused marital problems. Whereas prior
to this incident, Sheng reports a "peaceful" relationship
with her husband, she now has been unable to have sexual relations. She stated that if her husband reaches out to
show any type of affection, such as placing his arms
around her, she gets angry. She wishes to leave everyone
and isolate herself. Sometimes she wishes the children
could live with her parents. She feels frustrated because
she is unable to help her children with their basic tasks.
Sheng denies any suicidal ideation and states that her
children, her husband, and her family members give her
strength to live.

PIE Assessment

Your assessment is that Sheng is experiencing a number of
role problems including Paid Worker Role, Spouse Role,
and Parent Role. The incident with her employer occurred
just over six months ago, so the duration rating is 3. You
determine that her coping in this role is inadequate. In
addition, the harassment and being fired has also affected
her Spousal Role as well as her Parental Role. This client's
Factor I statement would be written as follows:

Factor I   Paid Worker Role Problem,
            Victimization type, high severity, 6 to -
            12 months' duration, somewhat inade-
            quate coping skills.

            Spouse Role Problem, Responsibility
            type, moderate severity, 6 to 12
            months' duration, somewhat inadequate
            coping skills, 1 to 4 weeks duration.

            Parent Role, Responsibility type, mod-
            erate severity, 6 to 12 months' duration,
            somewhat inadequate coping

With regard to Social Role Functioning Strengths,
there are several notable strengths. Sheng's relationship
with her husband and with her children until this incident
had been very positive and supportive. In addition, Sheng
has a large supportive family network upon whom she can
rely for help.

You determine that there are no environmental fac-
tors affecting Sheng's Paid Worker Role- Problem, or her
Spousal Role and Parent Role Problem. There are a num-
ber of employment opportunities in her community and
Sheng is well qualified to obtain employment. Her Factor
II statement would appear as follows:

Factor II   No problem.

Factor III

Axis I   296.23   Major Depression, single
episode, severe (principal
diagnosis).

Axis II   V71.09   No diagnosis on Axis II

Factor IV   Migraine headaches
(as reported by client)

This client's complete PIE description
would appear as follows:

Factor I   Paid Worker Role, Economic Problem,
Victimization type, high severity, 6 to
12 months' duration, somewhat inadequate coping skills.

Spouse Role Problem, Responsibility
type, moderate severity, 6 to 12
months' duration, somewhat inadequate
coping skills, 1 to 4 weeks' duration.

Parent Role, Responsibility type, moderate severity, 6 to 12 months' duration,
somewhat inadequate coping.

Notable strengths: Spousal Role and
Parent Role

Factor II   No problem.

Factor III

Axis I   296.23   Major Depression, single
episode, severe (principal
diagnosis).

Axis II   V71.09   No diagnosis on Axis II

Factor IV   Migraine headaches
(as reported by client)

Developmental Disabilities

Jim is a 49-year-old mild mentally retarded man who has
been attending the local regional center for developmental-
ly delayed individuals for the past 20 years. The center is
a day program and offers community activities and support
to its members. Jim is obese and suffers from epilepsy. The
epilepsy is fairly well-controlled through medication,

however his obesity has caused swelling in his joints, gout,
and borderline diabetes. He experiences chronic pain in his
joints and muscles as a result of the obesity.

Jim has lived with his widowed mother all his life,
but one week ago his mother died. No one in his extended
family can take him in, and there is no opening in the one
group home in his community.

PIE Assessment

You determine that the loss of Jim's mother is causing a
ChildRole(Adult) Problem, Loss type. This problem is of
high severity (4), the duration is two weeks or less (duration
= 5), and Jim has inadequate coping skills (coping index = 5).
This client's Factor I statement would appear as follows:

Factor I   Child Role (Adult) Problem, Loss type,
high severity, two weeks' or less duration, inadequate coping skills.

No one in Jim's extended family can take him in,
and there is no opening in the one group home in his community. You rate this client's Health, Safety, and Social
Services System Problem as high (4), and you determine
that there has been a severe lack of group homes available
for individuals with developmental delays in this community, but Jim has been experiencing this problem for one to
four weeks' (duration = 5). This man's Factor II statement
would appear as follows:

Factor II   Health, Safety, and Social Services
System Problem, absence of adequate
social services, high severity, 1-4 weeks'
duration.

Because Jim is experiencing some symptoms of
depression and anxiety related to the death of his mother,
he meets the criteria for Adjustment Disorder with Mixed
Depression and Anxiety. Also, Jim has been diagnosed
with mild Mental Retardation, thus his Factor III would
appear as follows:

Factor III

Axis I   Adjustment Disorder with mixed
depression and anxiety.

Axis II   Mental Retardation, mild.

Jim has several physical disorders that are affecting
his current situation. Factor IV statement would appear as
follows:

Factor IV   Epilepsy, obesity, gout, and borderline diabetes (as reported in medical records)

A complete multifactorial PIE report on this client would appear as follows:

Factor I   Child Role (Adult) Problem, Loss type, high severity, two

weeks' or less duration, inadequate coping skills.

Factor II   Health, Safety, and Social Services System Problem, absence of adequate social services, high severity, 1 to 4 weeks' duration.

Factor III

Axis I   Adjustment Disorder with mixed depression and anxiety.

Axis II   Mental Retardation, mild.

Factor IV   Epilepsy, obesity, gout, and borderline diabetes (as reported in medical records), severity = moderate, duration = 5+ years.

Substance abuse treatment

Holly is a 45-year-old woman who lost her husband through a sudden death approximately one year ago. As a child, she experienced sexual abuse perpetrated by her father and developed a substance abuse problem (heroin) which lasted from age 16 through age 36. She became sober after she met her husband at about age 37. The unexpected death of her husband one year ago, however, prompted a relapse. She first started drinking and shortly thereafter began using heroin again. Her drug use led to her unemployment six months ago, and she was forced to move from her home, as she did not have the resources to pay the bills. She became homeless for several weeks and was arrested for soliciting. She then entered a 21-day detoxification program. When the 21-day program ends, Holly plans to attend the outpatient methadone maintenance treatment program. She then hopes to find housing, become reinvolved with her sober supports and work on her bereavement issues as well as childhood abuse issues. Holly also hopes to return to work in the near future.

PIE Assessment

Holly is experiencing a number of Social Role Problems. One of her primary problems is the sudden death of her husband who was her major support—Spousal Role Problem, Loss type, high severity. His death occurred over one year ago, so the duration rating is 2. You determine that her coping in this area is inadequate. Although the client is presently in a residential substance abuse treatment program, she is doing well and there are no problems regarding her Inpatient Role. A secondary problem is her loss of a job six months ago due to her substance abuse. Presently, this is not a priority. Holly does wish to find employment, but when she is more stabilized. This client's Factor I statement would be written as follows:

Factor I   Spouse Role Problem, loss type, high severity, 1 to 5 years' duration, inadequate coping skills.

Paid Worker Role Problem, loss type, moderate severity, 6 to 12 months' duration, inadequate coping skills

You determine that there are several environmental conditions affecting Holly's situation. She has no health insurance, but is eligible for Medicaid. In addition, there is no cost for the 21-day detox program and the methadone maintenance treatment program is covered by Medicaid. These may be considered community assets or resources. There is, however, a dearth of safe, low-income housing in her community, which Holly has been experiencing for 6 to 12 months (duration = 3). Thus, her Factor II statement would be described as

Factor II   Basic Needs System: Lack of affordable housing, high severity, 6 to 12 months .

Holly's primary problem is her Substance Dependence. In addition, she is also experiencing a number of unresolved feelings following the unexpected death of her husband—Bereavement. She coped with his death by using drugs rather than dealing with her feelings of loss. You also determine that she experiences numerous long-term symptoms of PTSD due the sexual abuse she experienced in her childhood. Her Factor III statement would be described as follows:

Factor III

Axis I   304.00   Substance dependence—heroin

V62.82   Bereavement following
                death of spouse.

        309.81 PTSD, chronic

Axis II V71.09 No diagnosis on Axis II.

Factor IV None reported

REFERENCE

American Psychiatric Association. (2000). *Diagnostic and statistical manual of mental disorders*—4th ed.–text rev. Washington, DC: American Psychiatric Press.

Person-In-Environment (CompuPIE) System CD Installation Instructions

System Requirements

- The fanciest **software** requirement you will need to run CompuPIE is **Microsoft Access 2000 or later**.

- The remainder of the system requirements are basic:
  - PC with Pentium 75 Mhz or higher. CompuPIE is not available for Mac format.
  - Microsoft Windows 98 or later operating system
  - 256 megabytes of RAM (random access memory).
  - At least 20 Megabytes of hard **drive** space
  - A CD drive

- A printer (either local or network) if you wish to view or print reports. A printer driver is sufficient. (This is a requirement when using Access.)

  1. **Installation Steps** Insert CompuPIE™ CD into CD drive.

  2. Locate and open your CD drive.

  3. Copy the CompuPIE.mdb file from the CD to your hard drive. You can copy to the desktop or to a folder of your choice

  4. After you have successfully copied CompuPie to your computer, double click on it to open.

  5. Once you are running CompuPIE, click on the "Display Instructions" button at the bottom of the initial CompuPIE menu for further directions on how to use CompuPIE.

List of Interventions

Interventions Focused on the Individual—Targeting Factors I and Factor III

Art therapy

Assertiveness training

Anger management

Bibliotherapy

Behavior therapy

Career counseling

Cognitive therapy

Cognitive restructuring

Crisis Intervention

EMDR (eye movement desensitization reprocessing)

Existential therapy

Expressive therapies

Empowerment approach

Feminist therapy

Gestalt therapy

Guided imagery

Genetic counseling

Grief work

Hypnotherapy

Imagery relaxation therapy

Implosive therapy

Individual psychotherapy (for example, Adlerian, Attachment, Ego psychology, Jungian, Humanistic; Person centered, and so forth)

Inpatient treatment/hospitalization

Journal writing

Mindfulness/ focusing

Modeling and role-playing

Narrative therapy

Problem solving approach

Psychoanalysis

Psychodynamic

Psychotropic medications

Paradoxical intention

Rational emotive therapy

Reality therapy

Residential treatment

Sex education/Sex therapy

Solution focused

Spiritual counseling

Systematic sensitization

Stress management

Transactional analysis

Task centered approach/task assignment

Vocational guidance

Vocational rehabilitation

Interventions Focused on Families and Groups Targeting Factor I or Factor III

Communication training

Conjoint therapy

Couples/marital treatment

Divorce therapy

Family treatment/family therapy

Family life education

    Behavioral family therapy

    Bowenian

Experiential family therapy

Strategic family therapy

Structural family therapy

Narrative family therapy

Social constructionism family therapy

Brief family therapy

Feminist family therapy

Solution focused

Foster care (adult and child)

Group work

    Self-help

    Support group

    Psychodynamic group

    Interpersonal group treatment

Mediation

Milieu therapy

Multiple impact therapy

Network therapy

Parent training

Psychodrama

Sibling therapy

Social skills training

Interventions Targeting Environmental Problems— Factor II

Active resistance

Bargaining

Boycott

Case advocacy

Client advocacy

Community organizing

Confrontation

Consultation

Cooptation

Day care

Developing therapeutic milieu

Community education

Forming alliances

Interpretation to community or influential

Mediation

Negotiation

Networking

Ombudsperson intervention

Passive resistance

Placement facilitation

Political action

Use of influentials

Use of mass media

Numerical Coding

To record assessment findings PIE uses several methods. There is the long-hand system using PIE language (for example, Spouse Role Problem, Power Type, Low Severity, 1 to 5 years' duration, above average coping ability, Notable Strength. There is shorthand written version using the letters and numbers listed in the Indices (for example, Spouse Role, PWR, L, Y: 1-5, B, N. A third method uses a numerical coding system designed for those practitioners, researchers, or administrators who may wish to collect, store, or analyze case findings. Using the numeric coding system that same spouse role problem is coded: 1201.2221

Numerical Coding: Factor I

On Factor I each finding can be described in eight digits encompassing (1) The **Problem** (two digits), (2) the **type** (two digits), the **severity** (one digit), the **duration** (one digit), the client's **coping ability** (one digit) , and **other strengths** (one digit). Since the last four digits are qualifiers or descriptors of the problem, they are separated from the problem and type by a decimal point. The list of Problems, types and their codes are listed below.

Social role and relationship problem is designated by a two-digit number. For example, in the eight-digit array a Parent Role Problem is **11_ _, _ _ _ _** and a Spouse Role Problem is **12_ _. _ _ _ _** The type of role problem is recorded in the next two digits; for example, the Power type is **_ _ 10._ _ _ _** and Ambivalence type is **_ _ 20._ _ _ _**. Thus, a social role problem can be written and numerically coded by combining the social role code and the type of role problem code, for example, Parent Role Problem, Power type, **1110._ _ _ _** , Lover Role Problem, Ambivalence type is **2120._ _ _ _** .

The first digit to the right of the decimal point designates the **severity** of the problem. A Lover Role Problem, Ambivalence type of **high severity** (4 on a five point scale) is coded 21020.**4**_ _ . The second digit to the right designates the duration of the problem. A Lover Role Problem, Ambivalence type of high severity of **recent onset** (1 to 4 weeks or 5 on a five-point scale) is coded 2120.4**5**_) . The third digit to the right designates the **coping ability** of the client using a five-point scale with an option to postpone. A client with a Lover Role Problem, Ambivalence type, of high severity, recent onset and with adequate coping ability (3 on the index) would be coded 2120,45**3** . The fourth digit to the right indicates the presence of other strengths. A client with notable strengths (see chapter 8 for elaboration) would be coded **1** from the Strengths Index. Thus, a client with a Lover Role Problem, Ambivalence type, of high severity, recent onset, moderate coping ability, and with notable strengths would be coded 2102.453**1**.

FACTOR I	
Social Role and Relationship Problems	**Numerical Codes**
1. **Family Roles**	1000.
Parent	1100._ _ _
Spouse	1200._ _ _
Child (Adult)	1300._ _ _
Sibling	1400 ._ _ _
Extended Family	1500 ._ _ _
2. **Interpersonal Roles**	2000 ._ _ _
Lover	2100 ._ _ _
Friend	2200 ._ _ _
Neighbor	2300 ._ _ _
Member	2400 ._ _ _
Other	2500 ._ _ _
4. **Occupational Roles**	3000
Paid Worker	3100 ._ _ _
Homemaker	3200 ._ _ _
Volunteer	3300 ._ _ _
Student	3400 ._ _ _
Other	3500 ._ _ _
5. **Special Life Situation Roles**	4000._ _ _
Consumer	4100 ._ _ _
Caregiver	4200 ._ _ _
Inpatient Client	4300 ._ _ _
Outpatient client	4400 ._ _ _
Probationer/Parolee	4500 ._ _ _
Prisoner	4600 ._ _ _
Legal Immigrant	4700 ._ _ _
Undocumented Immigrant	4800._ _ _
Refugee Immigrant	4900 ._ _ _
Other	*4900._ _ _

Type of Problem	Numerical Codes
Power	_ _ 10._ _ _ _
Ambivalence	_ _ 20._ _ _ _
Responsibility	_ _ 30._ _ _ _
Dependency	_ _ 40._ _ _ _
Loss	_ _ 50._ _ _ _
Isolation	_ _ 60._ _ _ _
Oppression	_ _ 70._ _ _ _
Mixed	_ _ 80._ _ _ _
Other	_ _ 90._ _ _ _

Numerical Coding: Factor II

Coding for Factor II consist of five digits to the left of the decimal point indicating the **system** in which the problem is observed (two digits), the **type** (one digit) and the **specific problem** (two digits). Three digits to the right record the **severity**, **duration**, and other **strengths**.

A problem identified as a lack of adequate shelter in the community is first a Basic Needs System Problem (**05_** _ . _ _ _) The type of problem is Shelter (052_ _ . _ _). The specific problem is lack of available shelter on a regular basis (05**201**._ _ _). The problem is judged very high (4 on the five-point index) in severity (05201.4 _ _). The duration is 1 to 5 years (2 on the five-point scale). Coding now is 05201. 42_). The prospect of housing becoming available soon means possible strengths/resources (index code is 2) in the community. The complete code then is 05201.422: Basic Needs system problem, absence of shelter, a high severity problem of 1 to 5 years' duration with possible community strengths to help.

A problem is identified as lack of confidence in the police department to deal with attacks on gay males. The problem is reported by a client who was severely beaten. The client also states that this has been an issue for many years in his community. There is some prospect for change with a new police chief coming soon and a public education program regarding sexual identity.

This problem would be written in PIE language as follows: Justice and Legal System problem, justice and legal type, lack of confidence in police service, high in severity, duration of 1 to 5 years, possible community strength.

Using numerical codes the **System** category is **07_** _._ _ _ Judicial and Legal System. The **type** is Justice and

Legal, coded as 071_ _._ _ _ _ . Lack of confidence is a specific problem and is listed as 03 so the coding now reads 071**03**._ _. The **severity** is 3 on the severity index and the **duration** also 3 on the duration index. The code now reads 07103.**33** . The presence of possible strengths is noted on the third digit to the right. In this case it is 2 for **possible strength**. The numeric code describing the presenting problem for this would be 07103.33**2**. Translated back into PIE language this would read: Judicial and Legal system problem, justice legal type, lack of confidence in police services, high in severity and of 1 to 5 years in duration with some possible community strengths.

The discrimination issue is recorded as a separate problem. Discrimination is considered a **type** of Factor II Problem. It would be written in PIE language: Judicial and Legal **System** problem, Discrimination **type,** specific problem is Sexual Orientation, of high severity, 1 to 5 years' duration, and there are possible resources in the community. Coding would be 07 for Judicial Legal **System** 07**2** for **type** of problem (Discrimination), **06** for **specific problem** (sexual orientation discrimination). At this point the code reads: 07206._ _ _. The severity duration and resources are recorded to the right of the decimal point: 3 for high severity, 3 for duration, and 2 for possible resources. The numerical code then reads 07206.332.

Factor II Specific Problems

There are currently over 50 specific problems listed under Factor II ranging from "lack of regular food supply" to "excessively involved support system". These are listed in this Appendix and on the PIE System Worksheet. The compuPIE software automatically enters these and the other numeric code numbers.

FACTOR II	
Environmental Systems	**Numerical Codes**
1. BASIC NEEDS SYSTEM	05_ _ _ ._ _ _
Food/Nutrition	051_ _ ._ _ _
Shelter	052_ _ ._ _ _
Employment	053_ _ ._ _ _
Economic Resources	054_ _ ._ _ _
Transportation	055_ _ ._ _ _
Discrimination	056_ _ ._ _ _
2. EDUCATION &TRAINING SYSTEM	06_ _ _ ._ _ _
Education And Training	061_ _ _ ._ _ _
Discrimination	062_ _ ._ _ _
3. JUDICIAL AND LEGAL	07_ _ _ ._ _ _
Justice and Legal	071_ _ ._ _ _
Discrimination	072_ _ ._ _ _
4. HEALTH, SAFETY & SOCIAL SERVICES	08 _ _ ._ _ _
Health and Mental Health	081_ _ ._ _ _
Safely	082_ _ ._ _ _
Social Services	083_ _ ._ _ _
Discrimination	084_ _ ._ _ _
5. VOLUNTARY ASSOCIATION	09 _ _ ._ _ _
Religion	091_ _ ._ _ _
Community Groups	092_ _ ._ _ _
Discrimination	093_ _ ._ _ _
6. AFFECTIONAL SUPPORT SYSTEM	100_ _ ._ _ _
Affectional Support	101_ _ ._ _ _
Discrimination	102_ _ ._ _ _

FACTOR II	CODES
BASIC NEEDS SYSTEM PROBLEM	
FOOD/NUTRITION	05100
Lack of Regular Food Supply	05101
Lack of Food/Water Supply	05102
Nutritionally Inadequate Food Supply	05103
Other Food / Nutrition Problems	05104
SHELTER	05200
Absence of Shelter	05201
Substandard or Inadequate Shelter	05202
Other Shelter Problems	05203
EMPLOYMENT	05300
No Work available	05301
Insufficient employment	05302
Inappropriate employment	05303
Other employment problem	05304
ECONOMIC RESOURCES	05400
Insufficient Resources for Basic Sustenance	05401
Insufficient Resources to Provide Services	05402
Regulatory Barriers to Funds	05403
Other Economic Resource Problems	05404
TRANSPORTATION	05500
No Transportation	05501
Inadequate Transportation	05502
Other Transportation Problems	05503
EDUCATION/TRAINING	06100
Lack of Education or Training Facilities	06101
Lack of Adequate or Appropriate Facilities	06102
Lack of Culturally Relevant Facilities	06103
Regulatory Barriers to Services & Programs	06104
Absence of Support Services	06105
Other Education & Training Problem	06106

FACTOR II	CODES
JUDICIAL AND LEGAL	07100
Lack of Police Services	07101
Lack of Relevant Police Services	07102
Lack of Confidence in Police Services	07103
Lack of Adequate Prosecution/Defense	07104
Lack of Adequate Probation/Parole Services	07106
Other Judicial and Legal Problem	07106
HEALTH & SAFETY & SOCIAL SERVICES	
HEALTH/MENTAL HEALTH	08100
Absence of Adequate Health Services	08101
Regulatory Barriers to Health Services	08102
Inaccessibility of Health Services	08103
Absence of Support Services /Health Services	08104
Absence of Adequate Mental Health Services	08105
Regulatory Barriers to Mental Health Services	08106
Inaccessibility of Mental Health Services	08107
Absence of Support Services/Mental Health	08108
Other Health/Mental Health Problem	08109
SAFETY	08200
Violence or Crime in Neighborhood	08201
Unsafe Working Conditions	08202
Absence of Adequate Safety Services	08203
Unsafe Conditions in Home	08204
Natural Disaster	08205
Human-Created Disaster	08206
Other Safety Problem	08207
SOCIAL SERVICES	08300
Absence of Adequate Social Services	08301
Regulatory Barriers to Social Services	08302
Inaccessibility of Social Services	08303
Absence of Support Services/ Social Services	08304
Other Social Service Problem	08305

FACTOR II	CODES
VOLUNTARY ASSOCIATION	
RELIGIOUS GROUPS	09100
Lack of Religious Group of Choice	09101
Lack of Acceptance of Religious Values	09102
Other Religious Group Problem	09103
COMMUNITY GROUP PROBLEMS	09200
Lack of Comm. Support Group of Choice	09201
Lack of Acceptance of Com. Group of Choice	09202
Other Community Group Problem	09203
Religious Discrimination	09300
Community Group Discrimination	09300
AFFECTIONAL SUPPORT	10100
Absence of Affectional Support Systems	10101
Support System Inadequate for Affect. Reqs.	10102
Excessively Involved Support System	10103
Other Affectional Support Problem	10104
DISCRIMINATION	
Food/Nutrition Discrimination	05600
Shelter Discrimination	05600
Employment Discrimination	05600
Economic Resources Discrimination	05600
Transportation Discrimination	05600
Education/Training Discrimination	06200
Judicial and Legal Discrimination	07200
Health/Mental Health Discrimination	08400
Safety Discrimination	08400
Social Services Discrimination	08400
Religious Discrimination	09300
Community Group Discrimination	09300
Affectional Support Discrimination	10200

Numerical Coding: Factor III

Factor III uses the codes of the DSM or the International Classification of Functioning, Disability and Health (ICF) plus the PIE indicator for severity duration, coping ability, and strengths. The DSM Codes are available in the Diagnostic and Statistical Manual of Mental Disorders, Fourth Edition—Text Revision (2000) and the International Classification of Diseases (**Spell out and provide citation and reference at end of appendix**). Manual. DSM codes are programmed into the PIE software. The indicators are listed in the PIE Severity Index, Duration Index, Coping Index, and Strength Index

A client diagnosed by a licensed professional as suffering a major depression of moderate severity, with recent onset and demonstrating ability to seek and use help would be given the following numerical code: using the DSM: 296.22 (2,5,3,1).

Axis I: 296.22 = Major Depression, single episode

(**2** _ _ _) moderate severity

(2,**5**,_,_) recent onset of 1-4 weeks

(2,5,**3**,_) adequate coping ability

(2,5,3,**1**) notable strengths

Axis II: V71.09 = No diagnosis on Axis II

If a personality disorder were identified (borderline personality, for example) the coding would be F60.31 Borderline Personality Disorder

The severity, duration, coping ability, and strengths indicators would be used. Assuming that these were the same as for the Axis I diagnosis, the Axis II diagnosis would be coded: F60.31 (2,5,3,1)

Diagnoses by client report or from nonverifiable sources cannot be coded but can be listed as by client report.

Numeric Coding: Factor IV

Factor IV uses the codes of the ICD plus the PIE indicators for severity duration, coping ability and strengths. The ICD codes are available in the latest publication of the *International Classification of Diseases* (World Health Organization, 2007). (**Provide citation date and add reference at end of appendix**). Medical diagnosis should be noted as by a licensed health professional or by client report. Diagnoses by client report are not coded but may be listed in the PIE assessment

Examples of Factor IV Coding

Alzheimer's Disease is coded 331.0. If the problem is not yet severe and of recent onset with the client showing adequate coping ability with good support ,the PIE coding would be : 1 (low), 5 (recent onset),3 (adequate coping ability, 1 (notable strengths). The Factor IV code would read 331.0 (1, 5, 3, 1)

Multiple sclerosis is coded 340. Given the same indicator as in the first example the Factor IV coding would be 340 (1, 5, 3, 1)

Parkinson 's disease, primary, is coded 332.0. If present more than one year (2 on the Duration Index) and of high severity (3 on the Severity Index) and the client's ability to cope is inadequate (5 on the Coping Index) and there are some indicators of client strength (2 on the Strengths Index) the Factor IV code would read 332.0 (3, 2, 5, 2).

REFERENCES

American Psychiatric Association. (2000). *Diagnostic and statistical manual of mental disorders* (4th ed.–text rev.). Washington, DC: Author.

World Health Organization, (2007). *International classification of diseases-10 revision-clinical modification (ICD).* Available at http://www.who.int/classifications/apps/icd/icd10online/

World Health Organization. (2001). *International classification of functioning, disability and health (ICF).* Available from www.disabilitaincifre.it/documenti/ICF_18.pdf

Factor III Mental Health Conditions

The following is a list of Axis I mental conditions that can be used in Factor III

Academic Problem	V62.3	Amnestic Disorder NOS	294.8
Acculturation Problem	V62.4	Amphetamine Abuse	305.70
Acute Stress Disorder	308.3	Amphetamine Dependence	304.40
Adjustment Disorder Unspecified	309.9	Amphetamine Intoxication	292.89
Adjustment Disorder with Anxiety	309.24	Amphetamine Intoxication Delirium	292.81
Adjustment Disorder with Depressed Mood	309.0	Amphetamine Withdrawal	292.0
Adjustment Disorder with Disturbance of Conduct	309.3	Amphetamine-Induced Anxiety Disorder	292.89
		Amphetamine-Induced Mood Disorder	292.84
Adjustment Disorder with Mixed Anxiety and Depressed Mood	309.28	Amphetamine-Induced Psychotic Disorder, with Delusions	292.11
Adjustment Disorder with Mixed Disturbance of Emotions and Conduct	309.4	Amphetamine-Induced Psychotic Disorder, with Hallucinations	292.12
Adult Antisocial Behavior	V71.01	Amphetamine-Induced Sexual Dysfunction	292.89
Agoraphobia without History of Panic Disorder	300.22	Amphetamine-Induced Sleep Disorder	292.85
Alcohol Abuse	305.00	Amphetamine-Related Disorder NOS	292.9
Alcohol Dependence	303.90	Anorexia Nervosa	307.1
Alcohol Intoxication	303.00	Anxiety Disorder due to General Medical Condition	293.89
Alcohol Intoxication Delirium	291.0		
Alcohol Withdrawal	291.8	Anxiety Disorder NOS	300.00
Alcohol Withdrawal Delirium	291.0	Asperger's Disorder	299.80
Alcohol-Induced Anxiety Disorder	291.8	Attention-Deficit/Hyperactivity Disorder Combined Type	314.01
Alcohol-Induced Mood Disorder	291.8		
Alcohol-Induced Persisting Amnestic Disorder	291.1	Attention-Deficit/Hyperactivity Disorder NOS	314.9
Alcohol-Induced Persisting Dementia	291.2	Attention-Deficit/Hyperactivity Disorder Predominantly Inattentive Type	314.00
Alcohol-Induced Psychotic Disorder with Delusions	291.5	Attention-Deficit/Hyperactivity Disorder, Predominantly Hyperactive-Impulsive Type	314.01
Alcohol-Induced Psychotic Disorder with Hallucinations	291.3		
Alcohol-Induced Sexual Dysfunction	291.8	Autistic Disorder	299.00
Alcohol-Induced Sleep Disorder	291.82	Bereavement	V62.82
Alcohol-Related Disorder NOS	291.9	Bipolar Disorder NOS	296.80
Amnestic Disorder Due to General Medical Condition	294.0	Bipolar I Disorder Most Recent Episode Depressed in Full Remission	296.56

Bipolar I Disorder Most Recent Episode Depressed in Partial Remission	296.55
Bipolar I Disorder Most Recent Episode Depressed Mild	296.51
Bipolar I Disorder Most Recent Episode Depressed Moderate	296.52
Bipolar I Disorder Most Recent Episode Depressed Severe with Psychotic Features	296.54
Bipolar I Disorder Most Recent Episode Depressed Severe without Psychotic Features	296.53
Bipolar I Disorder Most Recent Episode Depressed Unspecified	296.50
Bipolar I Disorder Most Recent Episode Hypomanic	296.40
Bipolar I Disorder Most Recent Episode Manic in Full Remission	296.46
Bipolar I Disorder Most Recent Episode Manic in Partial Remission	296.45
Bipolar I Disorder Most Recent Episode Manic Mild	296.41
Bipolar I Disorder Most Recent Episode Manic Moderate	296.42
Bipolar I Disorder Most Recent Episode Manic Severe with Psychotic Features	296.44
Bipolar I Disorder Most Recent Episode Manic Severe without Psychotic Features	296.43
Bipolar I Disorder Most Recent Episode Manic, Unspecified	296.40
Bipolar I Disorder Most Recent Episode Mixed in Full Remission	296.66
Bipolar I Disorder Most Recent Episode Mixed In Partial Remission	296.65
Bipolar I Disorder Most Recent Episode Mixed Mild	296.61
Bipolar I Disorder Most Recent Episode Mixed Moderate	296.62
Bipolar I Disorder Most Recent Episode Mixed Severe with Psychotic Features	296.64
Bipolar I Disorder Most Recent Episode Mixed Severe without Psychotic Features	296.63
Bipolar I Disorder Most Recent Episode Mixed Unspecified	296.60
Bipolar I Disorder Single Manic Episode in Full Remission	296.06
Bipolar I Disorder Single Manic Episode in Partial Remission	296.05
Bipolar I Disorder Single Manic Episode Mild	296.01
Bipolar I Disorder Single Manic Episode Moderate	296.02
Bipolar I Disorder Single Manic Episode Severe with Psychotic Features	296.04
Bipolar I Disorder Single Manic Episode Severe without Psychotic Features	296.03
Bipolar I Disorder Single Manic Episode Unspecified	296.00
Bipolar I Disorder, Most Recent Episode Unspecified	296.7
Bipolar II Disorder	296.89
Body Dysmorphic Disorder	300.7
Borderline Intellectual Functioning	V62.89
Brief Psychotic Disorder	298.8
Bulimia Nervosa	307.51
Caffeine Intoxication	305.90
Caffeine-Induced Anxiety Disorder	292.89
Caffeine-Induced Sexual Dysfunction	292.89
Caffeine-Related Disorder NOS	292.9
Cannabis Abuse	305.20
Cannabis Dependence	304.30
Cannabis Intoxication	292.89
Cannabis Intoxication Delirium	292.81
Cannabis-Induced Anxiety Disorder	292.89
Cannabis-Induced Psychotic Disorder, with Delusions	292.11
Cannabis-Induced Psychotic Disorder, with Hallucinations	292.12
Cannabis-Related Disorder NOS	292.9
Catatonic Disorder Due to General Medical Condition	293.89
Child or Adolescent Antisocial Behavior	V71.02
Childhood Disintegrative Disorder	299.10
Chronic Motor or Vocal Tic Disorder	307.22
Circadian Rhythm Sleep Disorder	307.45
Cocaine Abuse	305.60
Cocaine Dependence	304.20
Cocaine Intoxication	292.89
Cocaine Intoxication Delirium	292.81
Cocaine Withdrawal	292.0
Cocaine-Induced Anxiety Disorder	292.89
Cocaine-Induced Mood Disorder	292.84
Cocaine-Induced Psychotic Disorder, with Delusions	292.11
Cocaine-Induced Psychotic Disorder, with Hallucinations	292.12
Cocaine-Induced Sexual Dysfunction	292.89
Cocaine-Induced Sleep Disorder	292.85
Cocaine-Related Disorder NOS	292.9
Cognitive Disorder NOS	294.9
Communication Disorder NOS	307.9
Conduct Disorder	312.8
Conversion Disorder	300.11

Delirium due to General Medical Condition	293.0	Factitious Disorder with Predominantly	
Delusional Disorder	297.1	Psychological Signs and Symptoms	300.16
Dementia due to Creutzfeldt-Jakob disease	290.10	Feeding Disorder of Infancy or Early Childhood	307.59
Dementia due to HIV Disease	294.9	Female Orgasmic Disorder	302.73
Dementia due to Pick's disease	290.10	Female Sexual Arousal Disorder	302.72
Dementia NOS	294.8	Fetishism	302.81
Dementia of the Alzheimer's Type	294.1	Frotteurism	302.89
Dementia of the Alzheimer's Type		Gender Identity Disorder in Adolescents	
with Early Onset Uncomplicated	290.10	or Adults	302.85
Dementia of the Alzheimer's Type		Gender Identity Disorder in Children	302.6
with Early Onset with Delirium	290.11	Gender Identity Disorder NOS	302.6
Dementia of the Alzheimer's Type		Generalized Anxiety Disorder	300.02
with Early Onset with Delusions	290.12	Hallucinogen Abuse	305.30
Dementia of the Alzheimer's Type		Hallucinogen Dependence	304.50
with Early Onset With Depressed Mood	290.13	Hallucinogen Intoxication	292.89
Dementia of the Alzheimer's Type		Hallucinogen Intoxication Delirium	292.81
with Late Onset Uncomplicated	290.0	Hallucinogen Persisting Perception Disorder	292.89
Dementia of the Alzheimer's Type		Hallucinogen-Induced Anxiety Disorder	292.89
with Late Onset with Delirium	290.3	Hallucinogen-Induced Mood Disorder	292.84
Dementia of the Alzheimer's Type		Hallucinogen-Induced Psychotic Disorder,	
with Late Onset with Delusions	290.20	with Delusions	292.11
Dementia of the Alzheimer's Type		Hallucinogen-Induced Psychotic Disorder,	
with Late Onset with Depressed Mood	290.21	with Hallucinations	292.12
Depersonalization Disorder	300.6	Hallucinogen-Related Disorder NOS	292.9
Depressive Disorder NOS	311	Hypersomnia Related to Axis I or Axis II	
Developmental Coordination Disorder	315.4	Disorder	307.44
Disorder of Infancy, Childhood,		Hypoactive Sexual Desire Disorder	302.71
or Adolescence NOS	313.9	Hypochondriasis	300.7
Disorder of Written Expression	315.2	Identity Problem	313.82
Disruptive Behavior Disorder NOS	312.9	Impulse-Control Disorder NOS	312.30
Dissociative Amnesia	300.12	Inhalant or Phencyclidine Dependence	304.60
Dissociative Disorder NOS	300.15	Inhalant Abuse	305.90
Dissociative Fugue	300.13	Inhalant Intoxication	292.89
Dissociative Identity Disorder	300.14	Inhalant Intoxication Delirium	292.81
Dyspareunia (Not due to a General		Inhalant-Induced Anxiety Disorder	292.89
Medical Condition)	302.76	Inhalant-Induced Mood Disorder	292.84
Dyssomnia NOS	307.47	Inhalant-Induced Persisting Dementia	292.82
Dysthymic Disorder	300.4	Inhalant-Induced Psychotic Disorder,	
Eating Disorder NOS	307.50	with Delusions	292.11
Encopresis without Constipation		Inhalant-Induced Psychotic Disorder,	
and Overflow Incontinence	307.7	with Hallucinations	292.12
Enuresis (Not due to a General Medical		Inhalant-Related Disorder NOS	292.9
Condition)	307.6	Insomnia Related to Axis I or Axis II Disorder	307.42
Exhibitionism	302.4	Intermittent Explosive Disorder	312.34
Expressive Language Disorder	315.31	Kleptomania	312.32
Factitious Disorder NOS	300.19	Learning Disorder NOS	315.9
Factitious Disorder with Combined		Major Depressive Disorder Recurrent	
Psychological and Physical Signs		in Full Remission	296.36
and Symptoms	300.19	Major Depressive Disorder Recurrent	
Factitious Disorder with Predominantly		in Partial Remission	296.35
Physical Signs and Symptoms	300.19	Major Depressive Disorder Recurrent Mild	296.31

Major Depressive Disorder Recurrent Moderate	296.32
Major Depressive Disorder Recurrent Severe with Psychotic Features	296.34
Major Depressive Disorder Recurrent Severe without Psychotic Features	296.33
Major Depressive Disorder Recurrent Unspecified	296.30
Major Depressive Disorder Single Episode in Full Remission	296.26
Major Depressive Disorder Single Episode In Partial Remission	296.25
Major Depressive Disorder Single Episode Mild	296.21
Major Depressive Disorder Single Episode Moderate	296.22
Major Depressive Disorder Single Episode Severe with Psychotic Features	296.24
Major Depressive Disorder Single Episode Severe without Psychotic Features	296.23
Major Depressive Disorder Single Episode Unspecified	296.20
Male Erectile Disorder	302.72
Male Orgasmic Disorder	302.74
Mathematics Disorder	315.1
Mental Disorder due to General Medical Condition	293.9
Mixed Receptive–Expressive Language Disorder	315.31
Mood Disorder due to General Medical Condition	293.83
Mood Disorder NOS	296.90
Neglect of Child	V61.21
Nicotine Dependence	305.10
Nicotine withdrawal	292.0
Nicotine-Related Disorder NOS	292.9
Nightmare Disorder	307.47
No Diagnosis on Axis II	V71.09
No Diagnosis or Condition on Axis I	V71.09
Obsessive–Compulsive Disorder	300.3
Occupational Problem	V62.2
Opioid Abuse	305.50
Opioid Dependence	304.00
Opioid Intoxication	292.89
Opioid Intoxication Delirium	292.81
Opioid withdrawal	292.0
Opioid-Induced Anxiety Disorder	292.89
Opioid-Induced Psychotic Disorder, with Delusions	292.11
Opioid-Induced Psychotic Disorder, with Hallucinations	292.12
Opioid-Induced Sexual Dysfunction	292.85
Opioid-Inhalant-Induced Mood Disorder	292.84

Opioid-Related Disorder NOS	292.9
Oppositional Defiant Disorder	313.81
Other (or Unknown) Substance Abuse	292.0
Other (or Unknown) Substance Abuse	305.90
Other (or Unknown) Substance Dependence	304.90
Other (or Unknown) Substance Intoxication	292.89
Other (or Unknown) Substance Intoxication Delirium	292.81
Other (or Unknown) Substance-Induced Anxiety Disorder	292.89
Other (or Unknown) Substance-Induced Mood Disorder	292.84
Other (or Unknown) Substance-Induced Psychotic Disorder, with delusions	292.11
Other (or Unknown) Substance-Induced Psychotic Disorder, with hallucinations	292.12
Other (or Unknown) Substance-Induced Sexual Dysfunction	292.89
Other (or Unknown) Substance-Induced Sleep Disorder	292.89
Other (or Unknown) Substance-Related Disorder NOS	292.9
Other (or Unknown) Substance-Induced Persisting Amnestic Disorder	292.83
Other (or Unknown) Substance-Induced Persisting Dementia	292.82
Pain Disorder Associated with Psychological Factors	307.80
Pain Disorder Associated with Psychological Factors and General Medical Condition	307.89
Panic Disorder with Agoraphobia	300.21
Panic Disorder without Agoraphobia	300.01
Paraphilia NOS	302.9
Parasomnia NOS	307.47
Parent–Child Relational Problem	V61.20
Partner Relational Problem	V61.1
Pathological Gambling	312.31
Pedophilia	302.2
Personality Change due to General Medical Condition	310.1
Pervasive Developmental Disorder NOS	299.80
Phase of Life Problem	V62.89
Phencyclidine Abuse	305.90
Phencyclidine Dependence	304.90
Phencyclidine Intoxication	292.89
Phencyclidine Intoxication Delirium	292.81
Phencyclidine-Induced Anxiety Disorder	292.89
Phencyclidine-Induced Mood Disorder	292.84
Phencyclidine-Induced Psychotic Disorder, with Delusions	292.11

The following is a list of Axis II mental conditions that can be used in Factor III

Antisocial Personality Disorder	301.7	Narcissistic Personality Disorder	301.81
Avoidant Personality Disorder	301.82	Obsessive–Compulsive Personality Disorder	301.4
Borderline Personality Disorder	301.83	Paranoid Personality Disorder	301.0
Dependent Personality Disorder	301.6	Personality Disorder NOS	301.9
Histrionic Personality Disorder	301.50	Profound Mental Retardation	318.2
Mental Retardation, Severity Unspecified	319	Schizoid Personality Disorder	301.20
Mild Mental Retardation	317	Schizotypal Personality Disorder	301.22
Moderate Mental Retardation	318.0	Severe Mental Retardation	318.1

Source: *Diagnostic and statistical manual of mental disorders,* 4th ed.–text rev. (2000). Washington, DC: American Psychiatric Association.

Factor IV Physical Health Conditions

The following is a list of medical conditions that can be used in Factor IV

Diseases of the Nervous System:

324.0	Abscess, intracranial		331.4	Hydrocephalus, obstructive
331.0	Alzheimer's disease		435.9	Ischemic attack, transient
437.0	Atherosclerosis, cerebral		046.1	Jakob-Creutzfeldt disease
354.0	Carpal tunnel syndrome		046.0	Kuru
354.4	Causalgia		046.3	Leukoencephalopathy, progressive multifocal
334.3	Cerebellar ataxia		330.1	Lipidosis, cerebral
850.9	Concussion		320.9	Meningitis, bacterial (due to unspecified bacterium)
851.80	Contusion, cerebral			
359.1	Dystrophy, Duchenne's muscular		321.0	Meningitis, cryptococcal
348.5	Edema, cerebral		54.72	Meningitis, herpes simplex virus
049.9	Encephalitis, viral		053.0	Meningitis, herpes zoster
572.2	Encephalopathy, hepatic		321.1	Meningitis, other fungal
437.2	Encephalopathy, hypertensive		094.2	Meningitis, syphilitic
348.39	Encephalopathy, unspecified		047.9	Meningitis, viral (due to unspecified virus)
345.10	Epilepsy, grand mal		346.00	Migraine, classical (with aura)
345.40	Epilepsy, partial, with impairment of consciousness (temporal lobe)		346.10	Migraine, common
			346.90	Migraine, unspecified
345.50	Epilepsy, partial, without impairment of consciousness (Jacksonian)		358.0	Myasthenia gravis
			350.1	Neuralgia, trigeminal
345.00	Epilepsy, petit mal (absences)		337.1	Neuropathy, peripheral autonomic
346.2	Headache, cluster		434.9	Occlusion, cerebral artery
432.0	Hemorrhage, extradural, nontraumatic		350.2	Pain, face, atypical
852.40	Hemorrhage, extradural, traumatic		351.0	Palsy, Bell's
431	Hemorrhage, intracerebral, nontraumatic		343.9	Palsy, cerebral
430	Hemorrhage, subarachnoid, nontraumatic		335.23	Palsy, pseudobulbar
852.00	Hemorrhage, subarachnoid, traumatic		046.2	Panencephalitis, subacute sclerosing
432.1	Hemorrhage, subdural, nontraumatic		094.1	Paresis, general
852.20	Hemorrhage, subdural, traumatic		332.0	Parkinson's disease, primary
333.4	Huntington's chorea		331.11	Pick's disease
331.3	Hydrocephalus, communicating		357.9	Polyneuropathy

348.2	Pseudotumor cerebri (benign intracranial hypertension)		345.7	Status, temporal lobe
335.2	Sclerosis, amyotrophic lateral		433.1	Stenosis, carotid artery, without cerebral infarction
340	Sclerosis, multiple (MS)		436	Stroke (CV A)
345.3	Status, grand mal		330.1	Tay-Sachs disease
345.2	Status, petit mal		333.1	Tremor, benign essential

Diseases of the Circulatory System:

413.9	Angina pectoris		403.91	Hypertensive renal disease with failure
424.1	Aortic valve disorder		403.90	Hypertensive renal disease without failure
440.9	Atherosclerosis		458.0	Hypotension, orthostatic
426.10	Block, atrioventricular		410.90	Infarction, myocardial, acute
426.3	Block, left bundle branch		424.0	Mitral valve insufficiency (nonrheumatic)
426.4	Block, right bundle branch		424.0	Mitral valve prolapse
427.5	Cardiac arrest		394.0	Mitral valve stenosis (rheumatic)
425.5	Cardiomyopathy, alcoholic		423.9	Pericarditis
425.4	Cardiomyopathy, idiopathic		443.9	Peripheral vascular disease
416.9	Chronic pulmonary heart disease		451.9	Phlebitis/thrombophlebitis
414.00	Coronary atherosclerosis		446.0	Polyarteritis nodosa
427.9	Dysrhythmia, cardiac, unspecified		427.60	Premature beats
415.19	Embolism, pulmonary		424.3	Pulmonary valve disease (nonrheumatic)
421.9	Endocarditis, bacterial		397.1	Pulmonary valve disease, rheumatic
428.0	Failure, congestive heart		427.0	Tachycardia, paroxysmal supraventricular
427.31	Fibrillation, atrial		427.2	Tachycardia, paroxysmal, unspecified
427 41	Fibrillation, ventricular		427.1	Tachycardia, ventricular (paroxysmal)
427.32	Flutter, atrial		424.2	Tricuspid valve disease (nonrheumatic)
427042	Flutter, ventricular		397.0	Tricuspid valve disease, rheumatic
455.6	Hemorrhoids		456.0	Varices, esophageal, with bleeding
401.9	Hypertension, essential		456.1	Varices, esophageal, without bleeding
402.91	Hypertensive heart disease with congestive heart failure		454.9	Varicose veins, lower extremities
402.90	Hypertensive heart disease without congestive heart failure			

Diseases of the Respiratory System:

513.0	Abscess of lung		518.81	Failure, respiratory
518.0	Atelectasis		505	Pneumoconiosis
493.20	Asthma, chronic obstructive		860.4	Pneumohemothorax, traumatic
493.90	Asthma, unspecified		483.0	Pneumonia, mycoplasma
494.1	Bronchiectasis, acute		482.9	Pneumonia, unspecified bacterial
466.0	Bronchitis, acute		481	Pneumonia, pneumococcal
491.21	Bronchitis, obstructive chronic (COPD), with acute exacerbation		136.3	Pneumonia, pneumocystis
491.2	Bronchitis, obstructive chronic (COPD), without acute exacerbation		482.30	Pneumonia, streptococcus
			486	Pneumonia, unspecified organism
			480.9	Pneumonia, viral
277.00	Cystic fibrosis		512.8	Pneumothorax, spontaneous
511.9	Effusion, pleural		860.0	Pneumothorax, traumatic
492.8	Emphysema		011.9	Tuberculosis, pulmonary

Neoplasms:

Note Some of the most common neoplasm codes are listed below.

228.02	Hemangioma of brain	197.5	Neoplasm, malignant, colon, secondary
201.90	Hodgkin's disease	171.9	Neoplasm, malignant, connective tissue, primary
176.9	Kaposi's sarcoma		
208.01	Leukemia, acute, in remission	150.9	Neoplasm, malignant, esophagus, primary
208.00	Leukemia, acute	152.9	Neoplasm, malignant, intestine, small, primary
208.11	Leukemia, chronic, in remission	189.0	Neoplasm, malignant, kidney, primary
208.10	Leukemia, chronic	155.0	Neoplasm, malignant, liver, primary
200.10	Lymphosarcoma	197.7	Neoplasm, malignant, liver, secondary
225.2	Meningioma (cerebral)	162.9	Neoplasm, malignant, lung, primary
203.01	Multiple myeloma, in remission	197.0	Neoplasm, malignant, lung, secondary
203.00	Multiple myeloma	196.9	Neoplasm, malignant, lymph nodes, secondary
225.0	Neoplasm, benign, of brain	172.9	Neoplasm, malignant, melanoma, primary
211.4	Neoplasm, benign, of colon	183.0	Neoplasm, malignant, ovary, primary
195.2	Neoplasm, malignant, abdominal cavity, primary	157.9	Neoplasm, malignant, pancreas, primary
		185	Neoplasm, malignant, prostate, primary
194.0	Neoplasm, malignant, adrenal gland, primary	154.1	Neoplasm, malignant, rectum, primary
188.9	Neoplasm, malignant, bladder, primary	173.9	Neoplasm, malignant, skin, primary
170.9	Neoplasm, malignant, bone, primary	151.9	Neoplasm, malignant, stomach, site unspecified, primary
198.5	Neoplasm, malignant, bone, secondary		
191.9	Neoplasm, malignant, brain, primary	186.9	Neoplasm, malignant, testis, primary
198.3	Neoplasm, malignant, brain, secondary	193	Neoplasm, malignant, thyroid, primary
174.9	Neoplasm, malignant, breast, female, primary	179	Neoplasm, malignant, uterus, primary
175.9	Neoplasm, malignant, breast, male, primary	237.70	Neurofibromatosis
162.9	Neoplasm, malignant, bronchus, primary	227.0	Pheochromocytoma, benign
180.9	Neoplasm, malignant, cervix, primary	194.0	Pheochromocytoma, malignant
153.9	Neoplasm, malignant, colon, primary	238.4	Polycythemia vera

Endocrine Diseases:

253.0	Acromegaly	252.0	Hyperparathyroidism
255.2	Adrenogenital disorder	252.1	Hypoparathyroidism
259.2	Carcinoid syndrome	244.9	Hypothyroidism, acquired
255.4	Corticoadrenal insufficiency	243	Hypothyroidism, congenital
255.0	Cushing's syndrome	259.9	Ovarian dysfunction
253.5	Diabetes insipidus	253.2	Panhypopituitarism
250.00	Diabetes mellitus, type/non-insulin-dependent	259.0	Sexual development and puberty, delayed
250.01	Diabetes mellitus, type I/insulin-dependent	259.1	Sexual development and puberty, precocious
253.3	Dwarfism, pituitary	257.9	Testicular dysfunction
241.9	Goiter, nontoxic nodular	245.9	Thyroiditis
240.9	Goiter, simple	242.9	Thyrotoxicosis
255.1	Hyperaldosteronism		

Nutritional Diseases:

265.0	Beriberi	269.3	Iodine deficiency
269.3	Calcium deficiency	260	Kwashiorkor
266.2	Folic acid deficiency	262	Malnutrition, protein-caloric, severe

261	Nutritional marasmus	266.2	Vitamin B_{12} deficiency
278.00	Obesity	267	Vitamin C deficiency
265.2	Pellagra (niacin deficiency)	268.9	Vitamin D deficiency
266	Riboflavin deficiency	269.1	Vitamin E deficiency
264.9	Vitamin A deficiency	269.0	Vitamin K deficiency
266.1	Vitamin B_6 deficiency		

Metabolic Diseases:

276.2	Acidosis	276.7	Hyperkalemia
276.3	Alkalosis	276.0	Hypematremia
277.3	Amyloidosis	275.41	Hypocalcemia
276.5	Depletion, volume (dehydration)	276.8	Hypokalemia
271.3	Disaccharide malabsorption (lactose intolerance)	276.1	Hyponatremia
276.9	Electrolyte imbalance	270.1	Phenylketonuria (PKU)
276.6	Fluid overload/retention	277.1	Porphyria
274.9	Gout	277.2	Lesch-Nyhan syndrome
275.0	Hemochromatosis	275.1	Wilson's disease
275.42	Hypercalcemia		

Diseases of the Digestive System:

540.9	Appendicitis, acute	571.40	Hepatitis, chronic
578.9	Bleeding, gastrointestinal	573.3	Hepatitis, toxic (includes drug induced)
575.0	Cholecystitis, acute	070.1	Hepatitis, viral A
575.11	Cholecystitis, chronic	070.30	Hepatitis, viral B
571.2	Cirrhosis, alcoholic	070.51	Hepatitis, viral C
556.9	Colitis, ulcerative	560.39	Impaction, fecal
564.0	Constipation	550.90	Inguinal hernia
555.9	Crohn's disease	564.1	Irritable bowel syndrome
009.2	Diarrhea, infectious	576.2	Obstruction, bile duct
558.9	Diarrhea, unspecified	560.9	Obstruction, intestinal
562.11	Diverticulitis of colon, unspecified	577.0	Pancreatitis, acute
562.13	Diverticulitis of colon, with hemorrhage	577.1	Pancreatitis, chronic
562.1	Diverticulosis of colon, unspecified	567.9	Peritonitis
562.12	Diverticulosis of colon, with hemorrhage	530.1	Reflux, esophageal
535.50	Duodenitis and gastritis	530.4	Rupture, esophageal
555.9	Enteritis, regional	530.3	Stricture, esophageal
535.50	Gastritis and duodenitis	532.30	Ulcer, duodenal, acute
558.9	Gastroenteritis	532.70	Ulcer, duodenal, chronic
530.1	Esophagitis	531.30	Ulcer, gastric, acute
571.1	Hepatitis, alcoholic, acute	531. 70	Ulcer, gastric, chronic

Genitourinary System Diseases:

596.4	Atonic bladder	592.9	Calculus, urinary, unspecified
592.0	Calculus, renal	595.9	Cystitis
592.1	Calculus, ureter	625.3	Dysmenorrhea

617.9	Endometriosis		607.3	Priapism
584.9	Failure, renal, acute		618.9	Prolapse, genital
585.8	Failure, renal, unspecified		601.9	Prostatitis
580.9	Glomerulonephritis, acute		585.1	Renal disease, Stage 1
600.00	Hypertrophy, prostatic, benign (BPH)		585.2	Renal disease, Stage 2
628.9	Infertility, female		585.3	Renal disease, Stage 3
606.9	Infertility, male		585.4	Renal disease, Stage 4
627.9	Menopausal or postmenopausal disorder		585.5	Renal disease, Stage 5
626.9	Menstruation, disorder of, and abnormal bleeding		585.6	Renal disease, End Stage
625.2	Mittelschmerz		593.3	Stricture, ureteral
620.2	Ovarian cyst		598.9	Stricture, urethral
614.9	Pelvic inflammatory disease (PID)		599.0	Urinary tract infection (UTI)

Hematological Diseases:

288.0	Agranulocytosis		283.19	Anemia, other autoimmune hemolytic
287.0	Allergic purpura		281.0	Anemia, pernicious
284.9	Anemia, aplastic		282.60	Anemia, sickle-cell
281.2	Anemia, folate-deficiency		286.9	Coagulation defects
283.9	Anemia, hemolytic, acquired		288.3	Eosinophilia
283.11	Anemia, hemolytic-uremic syndrome		282.49	Thalassemia
280.9	Anemia, iron-deficiency		287.5	Thrombocytopenia
283.1	Anemia, nonautoimmune hemolytic, unspecified			

Diseases of the Eye:

366.9	Cataract		377.30	Neuritis, optic
372.9	Conjunctiva disorder		379.50	Nystagmus
361.9	Detachment, retinal		377.00	Papilledema
365.9	Glaucoma		369.9	Visual loss

Diseases of the Ear, Nose, and Throat:

460	Common cold		477.9	Rhinitis, allergic
389.9	Hearing loss		461.9	Sinusitis, acute
464	Laryngitis, acute		473.9	Sinusitis, chronic
386.00	Meniere's disease		388.30	Tinnitus, unspecified
382.9	Otitis media		463	Tonsillitis, acute
462	Pharyngitis, acute			

Musculoskeletal System and Connective Tissue Diseases:

716.20	Arthritis, allergic		722.91	Disc disorder, intervertebral, cervical
711.90	Arthritis, infective		722.93	Disc disorder, intervertebral, lumbar
714.0	Arthritis, rheumatoid		722.92	Disc disorder, intervertebral, thoracic
733.40	Aseptic necrosis of bone		733.10	Fracture, pathological
710.3	Dermatomyositis		715.90	Osteoarthrosis (osteoarthritis)

730.20	Osteomyelitis		710.2	Sjogreri s disease
733.00	Osteoporosis		720.0	Spondylitis, ankylosing
710.1	Scleroderma (systemic sclerosis)		710.0	Systemic lupus erythematosus
737.3	Scoliosis			

Diseases of the Skin:

704.00	Alopecia		703.0	Ingrowing nail
692.9	Dermatitis, contact		701.4	Keloid scar
693.0	Dermatitis, due to substance (taken internally)		696.1	Psoriasis
682.9	Cellulitis, unspecified site		707.0	Ulcer, decubitus
695.1	Erythema muitiforme		708.0	Urticaria, allergic

Congenital Malformations, Deformations, and Chromosomal Abnormalities:

749.10	Cleft lip		741.90	Spina bifida
749.00	Cleft palate		750.5	Stenosis, congenital hypertrophic pyloric
758.3	Cri-du-chat syndrome (antimongolism)		760.71	Toxic effects of alcohol
758.0	Down syndrome		760.75	Toxic effects of cocaine
760.71	Fetal alcohol syndrome		760.73	Toxic effects of hallucinogens
751.3	Hirschsprung's disease (congenital colon dysfunction)		760.72	Toxic effects of narcotics
742.3	Hydrocephalus, congenital		760.7	Toxic effects of other substances (including medications)
752.7	Indeterminate sex and pseudohermaphroditism		759.5	Tuberous sclerosis
758.7	Klinefelter's syndrome		758.6	Turner's syndrome
759.82	Marfan's syndrome		752.51	Undescended testicle
742.1	Microcephalus			

Diseases of Pregnancy, Childbirth, and the Puerperium:

Partial listing of the most common conditions:			642.0	Pre-eclampsia, mild
642.00	Eclampsia		642.0	Pre-eclampsia, severe
643.0	Hyperemesis gravidarum, mild			
643.0	Hyperemesis gravidarum, with metabolic disturbance			

Infectious Diseases:

006.9	Amebiasis		99.41	Chlamydia trachomatis
112.5	Candidiasis, disseminated		001.9	Cholera
112.4	Candidiasis, lung		41.83	Clostridium perfrigens
112.0	Candidiasis, mouth		114.9	Coccidioidomycosis
112.2	Candidiasis, other urogenital sites		078.1	Condyloma acuminatum (viral warts)
112.3	Candidiasis, skin and nails		079.2	Coxsackie virus
112.9	Candidiasis, unspecified site		117.5	Cryptococcosis
112.1	Candidiasis, vulva and vagina		041.4	Escherichia coli (E. coli)

007.1	Giardiasis	41.81	Mycoplasma
098.2	Gonorrhea	041.2	Pneumococcus
041.5	Hemophilus influenzae (H. influenzae)	041.6	Proteus
070.1	Hepatitis, viral A	041.7	Pseudomonas
070.3	Hepatitis, viral B	071	Rabies
70.51	Hepatitis, viral C	056.9	Rubella
054.9	Herpes simplex	003.9	Salmonella
053.9	Herpes zoster	135	Sarcoidosis
115.9	Histoplasmosis	004.9	Shigellosis
042	HIV infection (symptomatic)	041.10	Staphylococcus
036.9	Infection, meningococcal	041.00	Streptococcus
079.99	Infection, viral, unspecified	097.9	Syphilis
487.1	Influenza, unspecified	082.9	Tick-borne rickettsioses
487.0	Influenza, with pneumonia	130.9	Toxoplasmosis
041.3	Klebsiella pneumoniae	124	Trichinosis
88.81	Lyme disease	131.9	Richomoniasis
084.6	Malaria	002	Typhoid fever
075	Mononucleosis	081.9	Typhus
072.9	Mumps		

Overdose:

The following is a partial listing. For additional codes for overdose/poisoning, see Alphabetic Index (Volume 2) of the full ICD-9-CM publication, under the table of drugs and chemicals.

965.4	Acetaminophen, overdose	969.6	Hallucinogens/cannabis, overdose
962	Adrenal cortical steroids, overdose	962.3	Insulin and antidiabetic agents, overdose
972.4	Amyl/butyl/nitrite, overdose	967.4	Methaqualone, overdose
962.1	Androgens and anabolic steroids, overdose	968.2	Nitrous oxide, overdose
971.1	Anticholinergics, overdose	970.1	Opioid antagonists, overdose
969	Antidepressants, overdose	965	Opioids, overdose
967	Barbiturates, overdose	967.2	Paraldehyde, overdose
969.4	Benzodiazepine-based tranquilizers, overdose	968.3	Phencyclidine, overdose
969.2	Butyrophenone-based tranquilizers, overdose	969.1	Phenothiazine-based tranquilizers, overdose
967.1	Chloral hydrate, overdose	965.1	Salicylates, overdose
968.5	Cocaine, overdose	970.9	Stimulants, overdose
967.5	Glutethimide, overdose	962.7	Thyroid and thyroid derivatives, overdose

Additional Codes for Medication-Induced Disorders

What follows is a partial listing of ICD-9-CM codes for Substance-Induced Disorders. These codes may be recorded as part of a DSM IV diagnosis when there is evidence that a medication, used at its prescribed dosage, has produced a Substance-Induced Delirium, Substance-Induced Persisting Dementia, Substance-Induced Persisting Amnestic Disorder, Substance-Induced Psychotic Disorder, Substance-Induced Mood Disorder, Substance-Induced Anxiety Disorder, Substance Induced Sexual Dysfunction, Substance-Induced Sleep Disorder, or a Medication-Induced Movement Disorder. According to the DSM-IV-Text Revision © (2000), the additional ICD-9-CM code should be recorded on DSM Axis I just after the 'Induced' Axis I psychiatric disorder.

Analgesics and Antipyretics, Substance-Induced Disorder:

E935.4 Acetaminophen/phenacetin

E935.1 Methadone

E935.6 Nonsteroidal anti-inflammatory agents

E935.2 Other narcotics (for example, codeine, meperidine)

E935.3 Salicylates (for example, aspirin)

Anticonvulsants, Substance-Induced Disorder:

E936.3 Carbamazepine

E936.2 Ethosuximide

E937.0 Phenobarbital

E936.1 Phenytoin

E936.3 Valproic acid

Antiparkinsonian Medications, Substance-Induced Disorder:

E936.4 Amantadine

E941.1 Benztropine

E933.0 Diphenhydramine

E936.4 L-dopa

Neuroleptic Medications, Substance-Induced Disorder:

E939.2 Butyrophenone-based neuroleptics (for example, haloperidol)

E939.3 Other neuroleptics

E939.1 Phenothiazine-based neuroleptics (for example, chlorpromazine)

Sedatives, Hypnotics and Anxiolytics, Substance-Induced Disorder:

E937.0 Barbiturates

E939.4 Benzodiazepine-based medications

E937.1 Chloral hydrate

E939.5 Hydroxyzine

E937.2 Paraldehyde

Other Psychotropic Medications, Substance-Induced Disorder:

E939.0 Antidepressants

E939.6 Cannabis

E940.1 Opiod antagonists

E939.7 Stimulants (excluding central appetite depressants)

Cardiovascular Medications, Substance-Induced Disorder:

E942.0 Antiarrhythmic medication (includes propranolol)

E942.2 Antilipemic and cholesterol-lowering medication

E942.1 Cardiac glycosides (for example, digitalis)

E942.4 Coronary vasodilators (for example, nitrates)

E942.3 Ganglion-blocking agents (pentamethonium)

E942.6 Other antihypertensive agents (for example, clonidine, guanethidine, reserpine)

E942.5 Other vasodilators (for example, hydralazine)

Primarily Systemic Agents, Substance-Induced Disorder:

E933.0 Antiallergic and antiemetic agent (excluding phenothiazines & hydroxyzine)

E941.1 Anticholinergics (for example, atropine) and spasmolytics

E934.2 Anticoagulants

E933.1 Antineoplastic and immunosuppressive drugs

E941.0 Cholinergics

E941.2 Sympathomimetics (adrenergics)

E933.5 Vitamins (excluding vitamin K)

Medications Acting on Muscles and Respiratory System, Induced Disorder:

E945.7 Antiasthmatics (aminophylline)

E945.4 Antitussives (for example, dextromethorphan)

E945.8 Other respiratory drugs

E945.0 Oxytocic agents (ergot alkaloids, prostaglandins)

E945.2 Skeletal muscle relaxants

E945.1 Smooth muscle relaxants

Substance-Hormones and their Synthetic Substitutes—Substance-Induced Disorder:

E932.0 Adrenal cortical steroids

E932.1 Anabolic steroids and androgens

E932.8 Antithyroid agents

E932.2 Ovarian hormones (includes oral contraceptives)

E932.7 Thyroid replacements

Diuretics, Mineral and Uric Acid Metabolism Drugs, Substance-Induced Disorder:

E944.2 Carbonic acid anhydrase inhibitors

E944.3 Chlorthiazides

E944.0 Mercurial diuretics

E944.4 Other diuretics (furosemide, ethacrynic acid)

E944.1 Purine derivative diuretics

E944.7 Uric acid metabolism drugs (probenecid)

Source: *International classification of diseases–10 revision–clinical modification (ICD)*. (2007). Geneva: World Health Organization

Frequently Asked Questions

The authors welcome comments and suggestions for improving the PIE System. They also will answer questions that the user may have. Questions may be submitted using the Web site www.CompuPIE.org

Frequently Asked Questions

What is PIE?

PIE is a system used by social workers and other human service providers for describing the problems presented by their adult clients. It identifies problems in the clients' functioning in social roles, problems in their communities, and with their physical and mental health. It is a tool for conducting and recording assessments, planning interventions, and evaluating outcomes. An holistic system, it includes assessment of client strengths. Its major purpose is to provide a comprehensive person-in-environment approach that will relieve, reduce or eliminate the problems the client is experiencing.

Why was PIE developed?

The PIE system was conceptualized and constructed under NASW auspices by a task force of practitioners and academicians. It provides an assessment system focused on social functioning rather than disease as in the DSM and other systems. It provides the human services practitioner an assessment tool that is comprehensive and yet easy to use in practice. It is used in all areas of practice—medical, psychiatric, family service, public welfare, employee assistance programs, private practice, criminal justice, and others.

PIE was also intended to help clarify the social worker's areas of expertise compared with those of other human service practitioners. The PIE system identifies problems in social functioning and problems in the environment (community) as social work's primary area of expertise. It identifies work with mental health and physical health problems as shared with other professions.

Who can use the system?

PIE is intended for use by practitioners, administrators, researchers, teachers, and students. Although not designed as a self-assessment tool it can be used in some cases by clients. All practitioners regardless of the theories of human behavior in which they were trained can use it. PIE is relatively culture free. It has been translated into French, Spanish, Hungarian, Japanese, Korean, Greek and is in use many other countries. around the world.

Can I get third party reimbursement using the PIE System? Can I use PIE instead of the DSM?

In the United States the DSM is the major system for third party payments at present, However most practitioners know its limitations in regard to treatment planning. The PIE System offers a more comprehensive view of the client's problems. It also includes a DSM diagnosis under its Factor III. There is no incompatibility between the systems and there have been PIE users who have submitted the more complete PIE assessment to payers with success.

Is PIE easy to learn? How can I get training in using PIE?

Using the Person-in-Environment System: The PIE Classification System for Social Functioning Problems (book) and the PIE Manual: Person-in-Environment System (manual) (Karls & Wandrei, 1994) (available from NASW Press at www.NASWPRESS.org) many are able to learn the system on their own. Many schools of social work in the United States and abroad offer training in the PIE system. Training in the PIE system is available in workshop format. Training outlines and recommendations are available in the PIE book. A six-hour workshop is usually sufficient to allow the practitioner to begin to use the system successfully. A self learning CD-ROM developed at the University of Calgary School of Social Work is available for those wanting to learn the system through their PC or MAC. Information on workshops or other interests regarding training can be obtained via the Internet at compuPIE @aol. com.

What are the advantages of using the PIE System?

PIE provides clear succinct statement about the various problems the client is presenting. PIE uses uniform language and format that allows case findings to be transmitted and understood by other practitioners and by clients. PIE produces findings that can be translated into clear comprehensive intervention plans.

How can PIE be used in administration and supervision?

Because client case data is collected in a uniform concise manner and is coded it can be easily summarized and reviewed by administrators and supervisors. Frequency and severity of client problems is easily obtained and can be used to see patterns of problems in the agency's clientele. For example it can tell the administrator the number of single homeless men who also suffer from various mental and physical disorders. It can tell how many female clients are suffering spousal abuse and also may be suffering various psychiatric and physical disorders. And it elicits intervention plans that can be quantified and monitored.

How can PIE be used in teaching?

For those teaching practice the PIE system helps the student understand and unravel the complex problem picture that many clients present. And it helps focus the student on his/her role in the helping process. It helps clarify the different roles played by other members of the helping professions

How can PIE be used in research?

Because PIE provides uniform data on client problems and is coded it serves as a natural ongoing research instrument that can answer many questions useful in policy development. It also provides a mechanism for testing interventions used in practice and can begin to provide answers to the question of what works best for whom?

What if I work primarily with children?

Although the PIE system was developed primarily to assess the problems of adults it has been effectively used with older children and emancipated adolescents. In cases of younger children using PIE to assess the problems of their parents or caretakers has proven very useful in developing intervention plans.

PIE in Other Languages

PIE in languages other than English

For the practitioner, teacher, student, and researcher it may be of interest to know that PIE has been translated from English into several languages. Information about the various translations can be obtained from the authors and publishers noted below.

French:

Ordre professionnel des travailleurs sociaux du Quebec
5757, Av. Decelles. Bureau 335,
Montreal (Quebec) H35 2C3, Canada

German:

Professor Stan Rethfeldt
University of Luneburg
E-mail: rethfeldt@gmx.de

Greek

Professor George Karpetis
Professor Theano Kalinikaki
Professo Alexandra Vergetis
Democritus University of Thrace
Department o fSocia lAdministration
1 P Tsaldari, Komotini 69100
Greece
E-mail: karpetis@otonet.gr: aleverg@TElIath.gr
Greek Letters: serie Social Work
E. Benaki 59
Athens 106 81, Greece

Hebrew:

Professor Yaron Yagil
Ramat Gan, Israel
E-mail: wendyc@sheba health.gov.il
There has been correspondence with other practitioners and teachers in other parts of the world who have been using PIE in the languages of their country. Among these are the Netherlands, Belgium, Italy and South Africa. Information on these can be obtained from the PIE Manual authors at compuPIE@aol.com

Hungarian:

Dr. Szabo Lajos,
Barczi College,
Social Workers Training Department,
Budapest, Hungary
E-mail: tailor@mail.digitel2002.hu

Jekli Sandor and Dr. Foldhazi Erzsebet
Csaladsegito Interzet (Family Help Center)
Eger, Deak Ferenc u.19, H- 3300 , Hungary
E-mail: csskeger@agria.hu

Japanese:

Professor Kyoko Miyaoka
Professor James Mandiberg
Aikawa Publishing Company
Toyota Building 2F
3-27-13 Koishikawa
Bunkyo –ku, Tokyo – to
Japan, 112-0002
E-mail: aikawabook@aol.com

Korean

Professor Sung-Jae hoi
Department of Social Welfare
Seoul National University
Nanam publication Company
URL: http:www.nanamcom.co.kr

Spanish:

Dr. Elizbeth Miranda
National Association of Social Workers
Puerto Rico Chapter
PO Box 192051
San Juan, Puerto Rico

PIE Assessments Using the PIE Worksheet and Using CompuPIE

This appendix provides two case examples, one using the PIE worksheets, the other using the CompuPIE program. The case of Martha Brown (see chapter 9, Family Service Agency for a discussion of this case) is presented on the PIE worksheet.

The completed worksheet illustrates how the social worker used the four Factors and designated the problem type, severity, duration, coping ability, and strengths for each of the relevant Factors to ensure a thorough assessment. The Assessment Summary and Intervention Plan sheets present a full summary of the assessment, the recommended interventions, and the priorities. Also, included are the social worker's clinical notes.

An assessment for Sam Palm has been generated using the CompuPIE program to create a PIE Assessment Summary (see chapter 9, Criminal Justice, for a discussion of this case). CompuPIE can also generate a longer, more detailed Assessment Summary. (Note: The CompuPIE software program also includes completed assessments and intervention plans for these two cases.)

PIE SYSTEM WORKSHEET

Client Name: Martha Brown

Client Alias:

Client Address: 3034 Albany Crescent, Los Angeles 93421

Phone Number: 213 444-4444

Practitioner: M. O'Keefe

Referred by: School Counselor

Assessment Date:

Assessed by:

Client I. D. #: 0001

Date of Birth: 1/2/1974

Gender: Female

Marital Status: Divorced

Ethnicity: Caucasian

Occupation: Clerical

Other Info:

FACTOR I: SOCIAL ROLE and RELATIONSHIP FUNCTIONING

PROBLEM IDENTIFICATION				STRENGTHS		INTERVENTION PLAN			
Role	Type	Severity	Duration	Coping Ability	Other Strengths	Goal	Intervention	Refer To	Expected Outcome
⊠ **Family**									
⊠ **Parent**	RES	M	Y: 1–5	4	Notable parenting strengths	1. Enhance parenting skills 2. Enhance family functioning 3. Reduce son's acting out behavior	1. Individual therapy 2. Conjoint and family therapy 3. Refer son for ind. therapy	Will see client Will see client Refer to Children's services	1. Ct. will implement a Beh mod program with son 2. Improved communication among family member 3. Son will begin ind. therapy
⊠ **Spouse**	MXD	M	Y: 1–5	4	Leaving abusive husband	Enhance ct's coping with divorce	1. Individual therapy 2. Possible group for battered women	Local battered women's shelter	Client will have increased knowledge of dynamics of DV and reduction of self blame
☐ **Child (Adult)**									
☐ **Sibling**									
☐ **Extended Family**									
☐ **Interpersonal**									
⊠ **Lover**	AMB	L	W 1–4	4		Help ct sort out feelings re relationship with boyfriend	Individual therapy	Will see client	Ct. will demonstrate enhanced choice making re relationship with boyfriend
☐ **Friend**									
☐ **Neighbor**									
☐ **Member**									

PROBLEM IDENTIFICATION				STRENGTHS		INTERVENTION PLAN			
Role	Type	Severity	Duration	Coping Ability	Other Strengths	Goal	Intervention	Refer To	Expected Outcome
☐ Other:									
☐ Occupational									
☐ Paid Worker									
☐ Homemaker									
☐ Volunteer									
☐ Student									
☐ Other:									
☐ Special Life Situation									
☐ Consumer									
☐ Caretaker									
☐ Inpatient Client									
☐ Outpatient Client									
☐ Probationer/ Parolee									
☐ Prisoner									
☐ Legal Immigrant									
☐ Undocumented Immigrant									
☐ Refugee Immigrant									
☐ Other:									

USE ABBREVIATIONS OR NUMBERS ON ASSESSMENT FORM

RELATIONSHIP TYPE INDEX

1	Power	PWR	6	Isolation	ISO
2	Ambivalence	AMB	7	Oppressed	OPR
3	Responsibility	RES	10	Mixed	MXD
4	Dependency	DEP	11	Undetermined	UND
5	Loss	LOS	12	Other (specify)	___

DURATION INDEX

1	5 or more years	Y: 5+
2	1–5 years	Y: 1–5
3	6–12 months	M: 6–12
4	1–6 months	M: 1–6
5	1–4 weeks	W: 1–4

SEVERITY INDEX

1	Low	L
2	Moderate	M
3	High	H
4	Very high	H+
5	Catastrophic	C

COPING INDEX

1	Outstanding	A
2	Above average	B
3	Adequate	C
4	Somewhat inadequate	D
5	Inadequate	F
6	Unable to judge at this time	I

STRENGTH INDEX

1	Notable Strengths	N
2	Possible strengths	P

FACTOR II: ENVIRONMENTAL SITUATIONS (SOCIAL SUPPORT SYSTEMS)

1. Basic Needs
2. Education and Training
3. Judicial and Legal
4. Health, Safety and Social Services
5. Voluntary Association
6. Affectional Support

1. BASIC NEEDS SYSTEM PROBLEM (Food, Shelter, Employment, Income, Transportation, Discrimination)

PROBLEM IDENTIFICATION				RESOURCES	IDENTIFICATION PLAN			
Type	Severity	Duration	Discrimination	Resource	Goal	Intervention	Refer To	Expected Outcome
☐ Food/Nutrition								
☐ Lack of regular food supply in community								
☐ Lack of food/water supply								
☐ Nutritionally inadequate food supply								
☐ Other:								
☐ Shelter								
☐ Absence of shelter								
☐ Substandard or inadequate shelter								
☐ Other:								
☐ Employment								
☐ No work available in community								
☐ Insufficient Employment								
☐ Inappropriate Employment								
☐ Other:								

PROBLEM IDENTIFICATION				RESOURCES	IDENTIFICATION PLAN			
Type	Severity	Duration	Discrimination	Resource	Goal	Intervention	Refer To	Expected Outcome
☒ Economic Resources								
☒ Insufficient resources for basic sustenance	M	W: 1–4		Undetermined	Improved clt's financial situation	Explore Community Resources	Refer to Legal aid re child support	Ct's financial problems will be alleviated.
☐ Insufficient resources to provide needed services								
☐ Regulatory barriers								
☐ Other:								
☐ Transportation								
☐ No transportation to job/needed services								
☐ Inadequate transportation								
☐ Other:								

2. EDUCATION AND TRAINING SYSTEM PROBLEM (Schools, Training Facilities)

PROBLEM IDENTIFICATION				RESOURCES	IDENTIFICATION PLAN			
Type	Severity	Duration	Discrimination	Resource	Goal	Intervention	Refer To	Expected Outcome
☐ Education and Training								
☐ Lack of education/ training facilities								
☐ Lack of adequate or appropriate facilities								
☐ Lack of culturally relevant facilities								
☐ Regulatory barriers								
☐ Absence of support services								
☐ Other:								

3. JUDICIAL AND LEGAL SYSTEM PROBLEM (Police, Courts, Prosecution/Defense, Probation/Parole, Detention Facilities)

PROBLEM IDENTIFICATION				RESOURCES	IDENTIFICATION PLAN			
Type	Severity	Duration	Discrimination	Resource	Goal	Intervention	Refer To	Expected Outcome
Justice and Legal System								
☐ Lack of police services								
☐ Lack of relevant police services								
☐ Lack of confidence in police services								
☐ Lack of adequate prosecution/defense								
☐ Lack of adequate probation/parole								
☐ Other:								

4. HEALTH, SAFETY, AND SOCIAL SERVICES SYSTEM PROBLEM

PROBLEM IDENTIFICATION				RESOURCES	IDENTIFICATION PLAN			
Type	Severity	Duration	Discrimination	Resource	Goal	Intervention	Refer To	Expected Outcome
Health/Mental Health								
☐ Absence of adequate health services								
☐ Regulatory barriers to health services								
☐ Inaccessibility of health services								
☐ Absence of support services/Health Services								
☐ Absence of adequate mental health services								
☐ Regulatory barriers to mental health services								

PROBLEM IDENTIFICATION				RESOURCES	IDENTIFICATION PLAN			
Type	Severity	Duration	Discrimination	Resource	Goal	Intervention	Refer To	Expected Outcome
☐ Inaccessibility of mental health services								
☐ Absence of support services/Mental health								
☐ Other:								
☐ Safety								
☐ Violence or crime in neighborhood								
☐ Unsafe working conditions								
☐ Unsafe conditions in home								
☐ Absence of adequate safety services								
☐ Natural disaster								
☐ Human-created disaster								
☐ Other:								
☐ Social Services								
☐ Absence of adequate social services								
☐ Regulatory barriers to social services								
☐ Inaccessibility of social services								
☐ Absence of support services/Social services								
☐ Other (specify):								

5. VOLUNTARY ASSOCIATION SYSTEM PROBLEM (Religious Organizations, Social Support Groups, Community Groups)

PROBLEM IDENTIFICATION				RESOURCES	IDENTIFICATION PLAN			
Type	Severity	Duration	Discrimination	Resource	Goal	Intervention	Refer To	Expected Outcome
☐ Religious Groups								
☐ Lack of religious group of choice								
☐ Lack of acceptance of religious values or beliefs								
☐ Other:								
☐ Community Groups								
☐ Lack of community support group of choice								
☐ Lack acceptance of community group of choice								
☐ Other:								

6. AFFECTIONAL SUPPORT SYSTEM PROBLEM (Family, Friends, Natural Helping Networks)

PROBLEM IDENTIFICATION				RESOURCES	IDENTIFICATION PLAN			
Type	Severity	Duration	Discrimination	Resource	Goal	Intervention	Refer To	Expected Outcome
☐ Affectional Support System								
☐ Absence of affectional support system								
☐ Support system inadequate to meet affectional needs								
☐ Excessively involved support system								
☐ Other:								

USE ABBREVIATIONS OR NUMBERS ON ASSESSMENT FORM

DURATION INDEX

1	5 or more years	Y: 5+
2	1–5 years	Y: 1–5
3	6–12 months	M: 6–12
4	1–6 months	M: 1–6
5	1–4 weeks	W: 1–4

SEVERITY INDEX

1	Low	L
2	Moderate	M
3	High	H
4	Very high	H+
5	Catastrophic	C

STRENGTH INDEX

| 1 | Notable Strengths | N |
| 2 | Possible strengths | P |

DISCRIMINATION INDEX

01	Age	AGE
02	Ethnicity, color, or language	ETH
03	Religion	RLG
04	Gender	GEN
05	Sexual orientation	SXR
06	Lifestyle	LIFE
07	Non Citizen	NCT
08	Veteran status	VET
09	Dependency status	DEP
10	Disability status	DIS
11	Marital status	MAR
12	Body size	BOD
13	Political affiliation	POL
14	Other:	

FACTOR III: MENTAL HEALTH CONDITIONS

	PROBLEM IDENTIFICATION				STRENGTHS		INTERVENTION PLAN			
Diagnosis	Professional Diagnosis	Client Report	Severity	Duration	Coping Ability	Other Strengths	Goal	Intervention	Refer To	Expected Outcome
DSM Axis I										
1. Major Depressive Disorder	Yes		M or 2	W: 1–4	4	Resilience, Knowledge/Intelligence	Decrease depressive symptoms	CBT therapy	Will see client for CBT Referral to Dr. K for possible meds.	Ct's depressive symptoms will decrease. Will demonstrate improved functioning (e.g., less time spent in bed)
2.										
DSM Axis II										
1.										
2.										
Other Diagnostic System Diagnosis:										
1.										
2.										

USE ABBREVIATIONS OR NUMBERS ON ASSESSMENT FORM

DURATION INDEX

1 5 or more years Y: 5+
2 1–5 years Y: 1–5
3 6–12 months M: 6–12
4 1–6 months M: 1–6
5 1–4 weeks W: 1–4

SEVERITY INDEX

1 Low L
2 Moderate M
3 High H
4 Very high H+
5 Catastrophic C

COPING INDEX

1 Outstanding A
2 Above average B
3 Adequate C
4 Somewhat inadequate D
5 Inadequate F
6 Unable to judge at this time I

STRENGTH INDEX

1 Notable Strengths N
2 Possible strengths P

FACTOR IV: PHYSICAL HEALTH CONDITIONS

	PROBLEM IDENTIFICATION				STRENGTHS		INTERVENTION PLAN			
Diagnosis	Professional Diagnosis	Client Report	Severity	Duration	Coping Ability	Other Strengths	Goal	Intervention	Refer To	Expected Outcome
Physical Health Conditions										
1. Frequent headaches		Yes	H or 3	M: 1–6	4		Determine etiology of headaches	Refer for Neuro-logical work up	St. Stephen's Neurological clinic	Understand cause of headaches. R/O any tumor, etc.
2.										
3.										
4.										
Other Conditions										
1.										
2.										

USE ABBREVIATIONS OR NUMBERS ON ASSESSMENT FORM

DURATION INDEX

1 5 or more years Y: 5+
2 1–5 years Y: 1–5
3 6–12 months M: 6–12
4 1–6 months M: 1–6
5 1–4 weeks W: 1–4

SEVERITY INDEX

1 Low L
2 Moderate M
3 High H
4 Very high H+
5 Catastrophic C

COPING INDEX

1 Outstanding A
2 Above average B
3 Adequate C
4 Somewhat inadequate D
5 Inadequate F
6 Unable to judge at this time I

STRENGTH INDEX

1 Notable Strengths N
2 Possible strengths P

ASSESSMENT SUMMARY & INTERVENTION PLAN

Client Name: Martha Brown

Client Alias: _____

Client Address: 3034 Albany Crescent, Los Angeles 93421

Phone Number: 213 444-4444

Practitioner: M. O'Keefe

Referred by: School Counselor

Client I. D. #: 0001

Date of Birth: 1/2/1974

Gender: Female

Marital Status: Divorced

Ethnicity: Caucasian

Occupation: Clerical

ASSESSMENT FINDINGS	RECOMMENDED INTERVENTION	PRIORITY
Factor I: Social Role and Relationship Functioning Problems		
1. Parent Role, Responsibility Type, Moderate Severity, 1–5 year Duration, Some-what Inadequate Coping Skills	1. Individual therapy 2. Conjoint and family therapy 3. Refer son for individual therapy	Medium
2. Spouse Role, Mixed Type, Moderate Severity, 1–5 Years Duration, Somewhat Inadequate Coping Skills	1. Individual therapy 2. Possible group for battered women	Medium
3. Lover Role Ambivalence Type, Low Severity, 1–4 Weeks Duration, Somewhat inadequate Coping Skills	Individual therapy	Low
Factor I: Social Role and Relationship Functioning Strengths		
Notable strengths in Parenting Role Notable strengths in Spousal Role—leaving abusive rel Notable strengths in Worker Role		
Factor II: Environmental Situations (Social Support Systems)		
Economic Resources: Insufficient Resources for Basic Sustenance, Moderate Severity, 1–4 Weeks Duration, Somewhat Inadequate Coping Skills	Explore Community Resources	High
Factor II: Environmental Situations (Social Support Systems) Strengths		
Undetermined		

ASSESSMENT FINDINGS	RECOMMENDED INTERVENTION	PRIORITY
Factor III: Mental Health Functioning		
DSM Axis I: Major Depressive Disorder: Single Episode; Moderate Severity, 1–4 Weeks Duration, Somewhat Inadequate Coping Skills	1. Individual CBT therapy Psychiatric evaluation for medication	High
DSM Axis II: No DX		
Other Diagnostic System Diagnosis:		
Factor III: Mental Health Functioning Strengths		
Resilience, Knowledge/Intelligence		
Factor IV: Physical Health Conditions		
Frequent Headaches, by Client Report, High Severity, 1-6 months duration, Somewhat inadequate Coping Skills	Referral for neurological workup	High
Factor IV: Physical Health Strengths		

CLINICAL NOTES / CLIENT DATA / CASE ANALYSIS / INTERPRETATION OF FINDINGS

Clinical Notes / Client Data / Case Analysis / Interpretation of Findings

Mrs. Brown a 33-year-old divorced mother of three children, was referred to a family services agency by a counselor at her son's school. Her eldest son, age 10, has been getting into fights more frequently at school, especially during the past several months. Mrs. Brown reported that her son has been difficult to manage since her divorce two years ago. She reported that he has frequent temper outbursts and bullies younger children and that these behaviors have also been increasing at home during the past several months. Mr. Brown reported a history of domestic violence in the marriage. She recently learned that her ex-husband is planning to remarry and believes that this may be one of the reasons for the increase in her son's behavior problems. Mrs. Brown also expressed concerned about her daughter, age 12, whom she describes as shy and doing poorly academically in school. Mrs. Brown reported that she is feeling overwhelmed and stated: "It is a struggle for me just to get up in the morning."

During the past three months Mrs. Brown has been dating a man whom she describes as kind, but added she does not know if she wants to continue this relationship because her son does not like him and this has contributed to arguments between her and her son.

Mrs. Brown's situation is aggravated by financial problems. Since her divorce she has had to move to a smaller apartment in a less desirable and less safe neighborhood. Her ex-husband pays only $200 a month in child support and he is sporadic in his payments. Also, one month ago due to cutbacks at her place of employment, her work hours were reduced to only 25 hours per week. She has been unable to find additional work and is worried about being able to make ends meet financially.

Mrs. Brown's mood was depressed during the interview. She cried during the session stating: "Life is just too much for me." She denies suicidal ideations stating she would never do that to her children. She is highly motivated and states she "wants to give her children a better life."

Case Assessment Using CompuPIE Short Form

Client: Palm, Sam   Assessed By: J. Karls   Assess Date: 12/5/2007

Case History, Dynamics and Comments

Sam is a 40-year-old African American parolee who was referred to our community agency by the social worker at the Adirondack Correctional Facility "so that we might help him with the re-entry process." After serving seven years in prison for a series of drug offenses and aggravated assault, Sam was released two weeks ago.

Sam resides at the local YMCA residential program, attends AA, and has found a temporary part-time job at a local restaurant. While in prison he obtained his GED and received training in auto mechanics, and he would like to find a mechanics job. Sam reports, however, that when prospective employers find out about his record, they don't hire him. He reports feeling a "lot of anxiety," but believes that he is turning his life around. He reports being drug free and wants to submit to random drug testing to prove himself. Sam has few social supports. He has no contact with his parents, who he described as physically abusive toward him as a child, and states that his old friends are all gang members, drug users, and "not worth knowing." His major support is his girlfriend, who visited him frequently while he was in prison. Another support he identifies is his Bible. Sam reports that after he gets a job and becomes more stable, he wants to begin a new life with his girlfriend.

	RECOMMENDATIONS	PRIORITY
Factor I: Social Role and Relationship Probationer/parolee role, Loss type, High Severity, 1–4 weeks duration, adequate coping skills	Weekly support group for recently released parolees	High
Factor II: Environmental Situations Shelter: Shelter discrimination–Other discrimination, High severity, 1–4 weeks duration Work/employment: Work/employment discrimination —Other discrimination, High severity, 1–4 weeks duration	Advocate for fair treatment of parolees in housing	
Factor III: Mental Health Functioning Axis I Diagnosis Substance abuse in remission, Moderate severity, 1–5 years duration, Above average coping skills Axis II Diagnosis No diagnosis on axis II	Write recommendation letters to potential Employers on behalf of client Referral to New Hope	High
Factor IV: Physical Health Condition Asthma, unspecified, Professional DX, Very high Severity, 5 or more years duration, Somewhat inadequate coping skills	Ensure client has access to needed medication and inhaler	High
Strengths and Resources *Factor I: Positive social relationships* Lover Notable strengths *Factor II: Environmental Resources* Parolee services *Factor III: Mental Health Functioning* Optimism, perseverance, spiritual awareness		

About the Authors

James M. Karls, PhD, LCSW, received a master's degree in social work at the University of Chicago and a doctorate from the University of Southern California. Over the past 59 years, Dr. Karls had an extensive career as a clinician, administrator, and teacher in social work. He started the first mental health clinic in California's Central Valley and directed mental health programs in California.

He held numerous appointed and elected offices within NASW, including the presidency of the California Chapter. Dr. Karls served on the national NASW Health/ Mental Health Commission and served as chair of the NASW Task Force on Standards for Case Management and the NASW Certification and Accreditation Commission.

One of Dr. Karls' key contributions to social work is his development of the "person-in-environment" (PIE) assessment system that attends more thoroughly to the biopsychosocial functioning than does the DSM. The first edition of the *Person-in-Environment System*, published by NASW Press has been translated in more than eight languages. Dr. Karls traveled extensively around the world teaching international social workers about the PIE assessment system.

Dr Karls received many awards for his contribution to the profession including NASW's Chapter and Unit Lifetime Achievement award. He was also honored by the NASW Foundation as a pioneer in recognition of exceptional contribution to the social work profession. In 2001 he received a Lifetime Achievement Award from the National Council for Community Behavioral Healthcare.

Dr. Karls founded the California Hall of Distinction that honors past and present great social workers in California and was himself inducted in 2008. The National Association of Social Workers Foundation honored Dr. Karls with the 2008 International Rhoda G. Sarnat Award.

James Karls died on June 29, 2008.

Maura E. O'Keefe, PhD, is an associate professor at California State University, Sacramento. Prior to this time she was a tenured associate professor at the University of Southern California, School of Social Work. Professor O'Keefe teaches advanced social work practice as well as human behavior and family violence. She has been a licensed clinical practitioner for more than 30 years and has worked with diverse populations in both urban and rural areas such as Brooklyn, New York; rural Maine; and the hill country of Texas. Dr. O'Keefe has worked in different capacities and settings, including community mental health centers, medical and psychiatric facilities, substance abuse programs, foster care and adoption services, as well as services for battered women and their children. She has a private psychotherapy practice in California.

Dr. O'Keefe has published numerous articles on family violence and has appeared as a consultant for on various television networks, including CNN. She has conducted research on child abuse and neglect, dating violence, battered women and their children, posttraumatic stress disorders, women and substance abuse, and the effects of exposure to family violence on children's adjustment. Additionally, she has conducted research evaluating the effectiveness of treatment programs on ameliorating some these problems. She has lectured on these topics at universities around the world.